INFLUENCING:
Marketing the Ideas That Matter

Chip R. Bell

Learning Concepts

INFLUENCING
Marketing the Ideas That Matter

Library of Congress Cataloging in Publication Data:

Bell, Chip R.
  Influencing—marketing the ideas that matter.

  Bibliography: p.
  1. Marketing.   I. Title.
HF5415.B4284   658.8   82-7772
ISBN 0-89384-051-3   AACR2

Learning Concepts
Austin, Texas

Distributed by University Associates, Inc.
8517 Production Avenue
P.O. Box 26240
San Diego, California 92126

Dedicated to the major Bells in my life:
Nancy, Bilijack, Ray, and Avis

PREVIEW

I am sometimes frustrated by having to read halfway through a book only to determine that it really wasn't for me. If this book isn't for you, I don't want you to experience that same thing. The next few pages, therefore, are designed to preview the coming attraction. Last time I checked, the preview goes on for 3 pages. Read them carefully. And, if you haven't already done so, thumb ahead to get a sense of how the book is organized and how it feels.

This book is about influencing effectively by using principles drawn from the field of marketing. While the techniques taken from the literature on power, communication, and selling can be potent, the use of marketing concepts affords a more comprehensive approach, allowing you to utilize a wider range of useful principles and practices. I intend to use *marketing* in the broadest sense of the word. Indeed, effective marketing encompasses the appropriate use of communication, power, and selling in order to influence and thereby achieve a particular outcome.

It *is* possible for you to influence the acceptance of ideas and decisions, and to shape the changes that occur in your organization. The rest of the book is devoted to describing how that can be accomplished and, what is equally important, how you can have a great time doing it.

Before now, concepts related to influencing others have been scattered throughout chapters of the personal and organizational effectiveness literature. I don't intend to rehash what you have read before—nor do I intend to quibble with it—but I will borrow from some of the richest sources, ones which have served me well. I hope you'll find the approach presented here to be valuable in increasing your confidence and competence as an idea-barterer in organizational life.

This book is first and foremost a planning tool, to enable you more successfully to compose and orchestrate your efforts when presenting ideas, leading people, managing projects, submitting budgets, and requesting additional resources. It is founded on the philosophy that mutual winning is not only possible, it is essential. Froth-at-the-mouth intimidators, beware! This book is not aimed at transforming its readers into dark, Machiavellian power brokers. Win-lose strategies sometimes promise short-term successes; they also risk serious long-term disasters. I have instead pursued a very positive perspective. I have found it is indeed possible to engage in, experience, and withdraw from an influencing problem, all the while witnessing the smiles of others and feeling your own. I believe this course is open to all who are sincerely interested in making a valued contribution to their organization's effectiveness.

Archimedes, the discoverer of the principle of leverage, said, "Give me a staff with length enough and a place whereupon to stand and I will move the world." The first goal of this book is to provide you with a long staff—a useful way of planning a strategy for successfully influencing decisions. Next, with a reassessment of your job role and its potential for contribution to organizational purpose—a revitalization of your "place whereupon to stand"—you will be in a position to move the world of organizational life and make that experience a winning one for all concerned.

This book will require more of you than your reading ability. It will engage you in an active way. You will come to the end of the book with a comprehensive plan for marketing your programs and proposals to those who will "purchase" them.

If you use this book effectively, this time next year you will have more program approvals to your credit, or more appropriate staff, or a more appropriate budget; in short, you will have been more successful in getting what you need to contribute to your organization in the way you desire. And, most important, it is likely that your organization will have been influenced to become more effective.

There are side benefits to taking this journey. I hope to present a perspective that will aid you in "seeing" aspects of organizational life that formerly may have been outside your frame of reference. "Seeing," as opposed to "looking," requires a sensitive combination of intuition, awareness, and vision. When you or I *look* at a landscape, we comprehend its main physical features; when an artist *sees* the same landscape, he or she appreciates it differently—at least, the artist experiences a deep sensitivity to color, form, tone, balance, and the like. A similar faculty can be acquired for seeing organizational life versus simply noticing it. This shift in perspective is a continuous challenge.

Influencing decisions is essential to the conduct of most middle- to upper-level job roles. "Seeing" entails gathering data which is sometimes elusive but frequently necessary for developing an effective influencing plan.

An analogy of the difference between looking and seeing would be to glance around a room with the purpose of quickly viewing everything. If you look a second time, this time viewing everything colored blue, the shift of reference points (from every thing to blue things) will enable you to see things you missed in the first viewing. By using marketing principles and techniques to influence the acceptance of ideas and their outcomes, this book will provide a different—a "blue-like"—frame of reference which should be useful in "seeing" previously unperceived aspects of the environment you will be influencing.

This book is a pragmatic blueprint for persuading decision makers. Its primary goal is to yield a recipe—a plan—for gaining decisions which favor you, as chef, and delight the consumer! In a parallel vein, the book is constructed to serve as an instruction manual for the realistic introduction and management of organizational change. Those who read closer may discover a pragmatic discussion on power within groups and a map for the effective avoidance of organization traps.

If you quickly thumb through the book, you will see pages with diagrams, boxes to be checked, and blanks to be filled in. Influencing is an experience, alive and vibrant. So, to use the language of human resource development, I prepared this instruction manual to be more experiential than didactic, more discovery-oriented than delivery-oriented.

If the book achieves its purpose, your copy will ultimately glisten with marginal notes and suffer dog-eared pages and wrinkled coffee stains. It is intended to be a working book, and I hope it evokes continual challenge rather than a single bedside reading. This working book is also meant to serve as a philosophical reference guide, and I trust you will unearth new insights with each reading. There are seeds of learning intentionally scattered throughout the text, seeds that can best grow only when you achieve a certain level of overall familiarity with the concepts. At some point, you may say, "Well, I didn't notice *that* the second time I read it!" My intent was to provide a message with significant depth and range. I opted to do this by writing in "stereo" rather than "long play." I trust you will experience the other tracks as you become familiar with the tune.

CONTENTS

1

GETTING ON BOARD WITH MARKETING

A friend once told me that those in positions with more responsibility than authority—be they financial specialists, first-line supervisors, personnel staff, or human resource development practitioners—would do well to have either marketing experience or a marketing planner in their units. At the time, I mentally labeled the comment an egotistical pearl of wisdom, because my friend was a marketing planner. Slowly, I began to realize my friend was on the right track: to operate successfully in today's organizations you should be able to think in marketing terms.

How many times have you heard people complain, or at least lament, that they felt frustrated by their too frequent inability to influence decision makers in their organizations? The halls, cafeterias, and lounges of many organizations are littered with comments like: "How can I sell that program to company managers?" "I'm having a difficult time getting a large enough budget or enough staff to do the kind of job that needs to be done," and "It seems to take forever to get an OK on the proposals I submit to top management."

The search for ways to influence within organizations is clearly not a new concern for people who must go up through the hierarchy for decision making. For years, we have acknowledged the need to be able to sell our ideas, proposals, budgets, recommendations, and requests for additional human and material resources to decision makers. We frequently say, "I need to sell my boss on that idea," "I'll have to talk the rest of the committee into this one," or "I'll have to take it to the Board." Ironically, we sometimes "win"—actually get a favorable decision—by the seat of our pants, or by our capacity to wing it. More often than not, our attempts to influence decision makers lack a coherent strategy—and we fail to get the outcome we sought.

The quest for effective influencing strategies often has led us to mine three bodies of knowledge. One mother lode has been the principles and techniques of effective communication.

> *"If I can actively listen to his critical Parent, by staying in my Adult while demonstrating unconditional positive regard, then he will...."*

Some communication approaches have ultimately been useful in increasing our skill at influencing others. Some approaches have not. Communication is only part of influencing. Influencing requires focused planning: much work must occur before the first words are spoken or sentence written.

Another body of knowledge some of us have hotly pursued is the principles of power and tactical negotiation.

> *"If I can manage to keep a sullen expression, wear a pin-striped navy blue suit, sit to his left, and act dumb when she asks about the shortfall, then I will...."*

The books that line our shelves attest to our infatuation with this vein. *Power: How to Get It/How to Use It, Success!, Winning through Intimidation, The Gamesman, You Can Negotiate Anything,* and *The Power Handbook* are but a small sample. Some have helped, some have not. And the perspective that some evoke for the individual in an organizational setting is to be questioned at least for its manipulative presumptuousness, and ultimately for its negative win-lose orientation.

The third area of knowledge to which some of us have turned for help in influencing has been that of sales strategies and skills.

> *"If I can use this priority feature to trump her benefit objection, while drawing on this proof statement, then I can...."*

We sit in on sales training courses designed by Wilson, Blodgett, Xerox, and Forum. Yet often, again, our batting average has not been perfect, and—where perfect batting is the objective—we continue to feel frustrated when we are unable to get approval for an idea or proposal. Like communication and power, selling presumes you know what to sell and how your idea, product, or service will satisfy a customer need. Effective selling requires the forethought associated with marketing.

I tapped all three bodies of knowledge in my roles as trainer, training manager, and internal consultant. I bought (and occasionally read and learned from) some of those same books, and I sat through the same seminars. Repeatedly, I found myself more exasperated than satisfied.

One day, it dawned on me: if giants like Procter & Gamble could effectively influence their markets, why couldn't I influence my own marketplace? I quickly called on my marketing planner friend and over a period of months gained the equivalent of a graduate education in a whole world I knew little about—using marketing principles to influence consumer behavior. Granted, my consumers were the managers and executives in my organization; yet, the principles promised potent application.

THE CONCEPT OF MARKETING

Procter & Gamble doesn't simply sell products, it markets them. This may sound like a semantics game to you at this point. I thought so too at first, but I learned otherwise.

While the words *selling* and *marketing* are cut from the same cloth, they refer to different activities and, more important, to different ways of viewing the act of influencing an outcome. Philosophically, selling is like a solo played by a violinist, while marketing is more like a symphony performed by an orchestra. Optimally, the solo is part of the symphony.

Selling is essentially the face-to-face interaction designed to enable two parties to exchange value for value. We do it all the time. Marketing is a larger process. While it encompasses the exchange, it begins long before folks are eyeball to eyeball. It entails analysis, planning, decision making, evaluating—a host of other rational, logical functions before the intuitive, interpersonal people-skills are called for.

By the sixties, the field of marketing began to be acknowledged as a specialized discipline, consisting of more than sales techniques and promotional tactics. Peter Drucker, Philip Kotler, and Theodore Levitt (currently professors at Claremont Graduate School, Northwestern University, and Harvard, respectively) were early leaders in forming much of our thinking about marketing.

In his book *Marketing Management*, Kotler eloquently outlines the age-old *sales concept* that focused on products or services as the first order of business.[1] Organizations that followed the sales concept got into business by identifying a product or service they wanted to sell

---

[1]Philip Kotler, *Marketing Management* (Englewood Cliffs, N.J.: Prentice-Hall, 1976).

and deploying resources to manufacture the product or provide the service. These organizations used selling and promotion as the primary means of acquainting the consumer with their product or service and measured their success through sales volume and profits. In effect, then, the sales concept was fulfilled by selling the inventory "by hook or by crook."

The sales concept may sound like a good one. In an era of limited choice, it worked fairly well. Organizations with products or services desired by the public succeeded. If the public lost interest in a product or service, the organization went under—the buggy whip manufacturer is the cliche.

The *marketing* (as opposed to sales) *concept* posited by Drucker, Kotler, Levitt, and others was born in the present era of abundant choice.[2] It shifted the organization's focus from its products or services to its consumers and their respective markets. The emphasis changed from "how can we get folks to buy our inventory of products and services?" to "*what do people want and how can we best respond to their needs?*"

Rather than depending solely on sales and promotion, the marketing concept calls for comprehensive market research and integrated product development and promotion. The functional areas of an organization are coordinated for maximum marketing impact— each area with the goal of aiding the organization in being perceived within its marketplace as distinctively competent in the products or services it offers. Organizations that operate with this viewpoint use a systematic planning process; their resources are focused on goals, strategies, and timely action plans which are evolved from a clear understanding of the organization's primary purpose. And the purpose is to serve their customers. Form follows function; action follows forethought.

Contemporary organizations that use the marketing concept measure "winning" in the profitability they enjoy *through attainment of satisfying customer relationships.* Maximum corporate energy is devoted to understanding the changing marketplace, assessing consumer needs and desires, and responding in ways valued by that consumer.

Corporate alignment with consumer needs and desires is axiomatic in a marketing-oriented organization. Read that line again—it will be a key thought woven throughout.

It is not surprising that the marketing concept surfaced when it did. Although we have a long way to go, the last thirty years have

---

[2]Others who contributed original work on the marketing concept included J.B. McKitterick, John Howard, Neil Borden, and Wroe Anderson.

witnessed a gradual alteration in the conventional view of business as a greedy, profits-at-all-costs enterprise. The last two decades have seen businesses demonstrate wider community interest, greater concern for employees, and a healthier respect for customers. The marketing concept is a fitting and timely approach to guiding the manner in which organizations influence their marketplaces.

The marketing concept can, likewise, be a fitting guide for how you influence your consumers—the managers and executives who must decide to "purchase" your proposal, idea, or request for a larger budget, different equipment , or additional staff.

In some ways, what follows resembles a cram course in marketing planning! I hope you will be surprised and pleased at how readily marketing principles can be employed to sharpen your influencing skills.

SELECTING A FRAMEWORK

As you have probably surmised from thumbing through the book, the approach I recommend will be fashioned around a conceptual framework, or model. (I will use the words *model* and *framework* interchangeably.) Models can be powerful aids in pointing to areas our minds should explore and in surfacing the gaps in our thinking which should be filled.

I believe people who must look to a higher authority to get programs, ideas, budgets, and proposals approved can use this model to influence their organizations more effectively. I believe the model will be particularly beneficial to those whose work involves initiating and implementing relatively large-scale changes in their organizations—line managers, supervisors, human resource development staff, personnel specialists, organization development staff. I will use the term *influencer* as a label for the assortment of people who might find this book useful. Since the lion's share of my experience is in the human resource development field, most of the examples in the text will come from this area.

Frameworks are essentially roadmaps to enable those travelling on the path to effectiveness to anticipate special vistas along the way. Frameworks also allow us to notice time without being a victim of time. They provide a structure which facilitates the release of insight and creativity.

A framework provides a recipe, in my way of thinking. I use the recipe analogy deliberately, because a recipe frees the cook from having to remember all the ingredients and allows innovation around how those ingredients are used. In other words, a person adapts the recipe—the model or framework—to his or her own taste. Also, as blueprints of the possible, recipes enable the user to readily identify gaps and problems that need to be addressed. Julia Child may have said, "If you didn't have a recipe, you probably wouldn't know you were out of vanilla."

The framework shown in figure 1 provides the basic roadmap for proceeding through the marketing approach to influencing decision makers in your organization. A quick perusal reveals the framework to be organized into five phases—the goal-setting phase, the assessment phase, the marketing solutions phase, the presentation phase, and the decision phase.

The *goal-setting* phase is principally concerned with articulating a role and mission. It involves both checking out our identity (who are we?) and defining a vision (who do we hope to be?).

The *assessment* phase is essentially market research—assessing *who* the consumer is, what the *characteristics* of the consumer are, plus identifying what the consumer *wants, needs,* or *values,* and in what *form.* Also assessed is the ability of the organization unit or individual to deliver on claims to provide certain levels of product or service quality. Emphasis is both on status quo assessment as well as forecasting.

The *marketing solutions* phase covers activities often labeled marketing planning. Marketing planning combines the information gathered through the assessment (market research) with the goals and objectives that have been set to forge a plan (strategy and tactics) for influencing the marketplace. The goal of marketing planning is to develop recommendations for improving the perception of distinctive competency which the marketplace has of the organization, the unit, or the individual.

The *presentation* phase corresponds to the actions performed by sales and advertising units. With the knowledge that the strategic plan meshes with the consumer's needs and the unit's goals, it is possible to devise promotional activities, decide on packaging, and create sales approaches. Selling efforts are planned and conducted within the parameters of the strategic marketing plan.

The *decision* phase is when the consumer decides to purchase or not purchase. There is much to be considered in this phase by the person doing the influencing. In your case, the consumer is one you will call on repeatedly. How you analyze the factors influencing your consumer's decisions can spell out *long-term* success or failure.

There are several steps associated with each phase. Some of the steps will occupy a complete chapter of this book; others, a portion of a chapter. For most steps, the narrative is accompanied by exercises or worksheets to aid you in guided thought. When you put your conclusions from them together, you will have devised a comprehen-

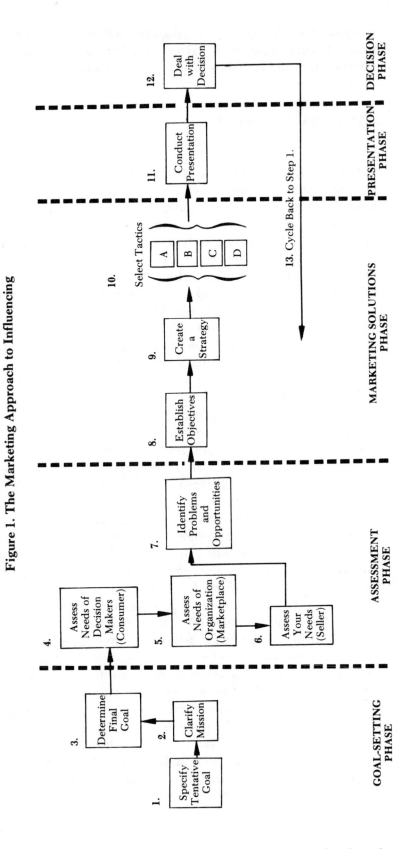

Figure 1. The Marketing Approach to Influencing

sive plan for influencing. As you go through the process in the future, practice will enable you to skip the background and explanation and go straight to the activities for forging your plan.

THE ROLE OF POWER

Power, according to psychologist Rollo May, is the ability to direct or prevent change. Earlier, when I described the relatively widespread tendency to search for influencing techniques in the realm of power, I specifically meant the coercive domain of intimidation and one-upmanship. Influencing clearly involves the use of power. However, effective influencing—causing an outcome to happen which *might* not have occurred without some effort by the influencer—can be accomplished without coercion and without resorting to intimidation tactics.

Influence and power normally are very similar concepts. Many view them as synonymous. I believe a book dealing with the skill of influencing would be incomplete without some discussion of power as it pertains to influencing. What may appear to be a small detour here is in actuality a part of the philosophical foundation for using the marketing model.

Two types of power exist in organizations—role power and personal power. *Role power* has to do with authority, status, rank, position—all executives, managers, legislators, shop stewards, principals, presidents, admirals, and so forth have such power. Whether they choose to use it is a different matter altogether. Role power is sometimes defined as the *right* to influence others.

Personal power is associated with one's self—one's style, charisma, talents, skills, traits, knowledge displayed with others. Some define personal power as the *ability* to influence others, entirely aside from the power bestowed by the organization. True leadership, incidentally, is associated less with role power and more with personal power.

Role power is created through structured relationships in organizations. It is assigned. Personal power, on the other hand, is rallied and directed from within one's self. It is directly related to how we manifest with other people and how we perceive individuals and groups. It is exercised through relationships and one's ability to influence, from within oneself, the purposes and actions of others.

The *possession* of a certain type of power—whether role or personal—is not really the issue in influencing. We *all* have personal power; many of us simply do not know how to employ it. This is primarily a function of awareness. Each of us also has role power, some more than others. And many of us have seen people abuse it. The crux of the power issue is whether we choose to use power appropriately.

Many first-line and middle managers, as well as staff people, rue their lack of sufficient role power. When we have little role power, I believe we must rely on the application of personal power for effectiveness. I hope to convey that the application of personal power is, in essence, a matter of personal growth. As you or I gain facility with personal power, we become more comfortable with ourselves. We, in turn, increase our ability to influence in our organizations and in other settings. The cycle continues, bolstering our self-esteem in the process.

I have sprinkled little cues on effectively using personal power throughout the remainder of this book. Only in a few places will you find them out in full view. More typically, they are carefully tucked under other ideas—part of the stereophonic message promised earlier.

GETTING SET TO INFLUENCE

You now know why this book was written and what it is designed to accomplish. If you have reached this point and have not laid it aside, I will assume you are in the right book and have identified your need as one which can be met by what is proposed. The strength of your agreement may range from a quiet "hmm, maybe so" to a resounding "absolutely!" No matter—just a bit of agreement is all that is required for a productive encounter.

I want you to feel like this is our book—yours and mine together. That we have the kind of relationship which allows us to talk freely to each other, to whisper and pass notes under the table so to speak. I plan to get quite personal with you: the process of planning an influence strategy will require deep thoughtfulness and demand broad thoroughness. It is my hope to help you acquire a depth of introspection (self-inspection) that will enable you to increase your personal power and enhance your professional effectiveness.

This book may test your patience. You might already feel yourself tugging at the reins, raring to lunge into the thick of marketing strategy and promotional tactics. Hold on! There were many ways to present this approach to influencing. I opted to unfold the recipe gradually, to enable you to fully experience each ingredient before moving to the next. The cake won't come out of the oven until you reach the end of the book. This is not a college outline series cram book, so get settled for a deliberate journey. By the same token, I do not aim to bore you—this is not *War and Peace*, and this *is* the only volume! Sit back at your desk or in your reading chair and relax.

In • flu • ence (in'floo-
ens), *n.*, *v.*, -enc • ing.

1. the process or
action of producing
effects on others by
indirect or intangible
means — *v.t.* 2. to
exercise influence on;
affect; sway. 3. to
move or impel (a
person) as to some
action. *Syn.* 4.
persuade, induce.

PART I

THE GOAL-SETTING PHASE

Many of us have gone about the act of influencing like the stereotypical public relations promoter—with flair and color, sound and fury. Often we have bagged more flak than game. A marketing approach to influencing cannot be achieved through a hair-triggered leap into tactics, or action plans. Such leaps may salve our impatience, but they risk missing the mark entirely.

Influencing requires considered efforts. We must be confident that our influencing activities are congruent with what is needed by the buyer and consonant with what we can deliver as seller. To achieve congruence and consonance, clear goals must be set and a comprehensive assessment conducted to determine what is appropriate for our marketplace.

As professionals in organizations, we *are* sellers of fitting ideas. As we do this, we must have two concerns. Is my idea of sufficient worth? Can I convince others of its worth? To put all our energy on one question to the exclusion of the other is to court failure.

There are some who think that the worth of their idea, proposal, or approach is the paramount concern. They might have the Ralph Waldo Emerson view—"If I build the best mousetrap ever, the world will beat a path to my door." Idea-focused people too often stand in a long line with the many great inventors who failed—in the practical sense—because they were unable to successfully market their good inventions.

Then there are people who think only of how to convince others, rather than putting a portion of their energy on getting a worthy idea. Their sole concern is with persuasion, promoting, hyping, or advertising. They are successful only for the first sale. They act as though they had never heard the famous marketing adage pertaining to dog food: "No matter how slick the advertising, how nutritional the contents, how clever the packaging, or how cheap the price, if the dogs won't eat it, the dog food won't sell"—at least, not more than once.

You must feel proud of your idea, proposal, budget, or request. You must also want to win at securing approval. The *blending* of appropriate creation with sound promotion is the stuff this book is made of.

The goal-setting phase contains three steps, as shown in the illustration below. Chapter 2 will lead you through them.

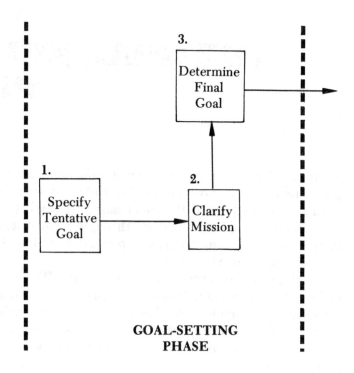

2

CLARIFYING MISSION AND GOAL

Do what you can with what you have,
where you are.

—Teddy Roosevelt

There is a familiar adage written years ago by Seneca that states, "If a captain does not know to which port his ship is sailing, all winds are favorable." Mission helps us clarify the reason for our actions; goals help identify their direction. In this chapter, we will explore both. Let's begin with where you are.

SPECIFYING A TENTATIVE GOAL

The place to begin is your thoughtful consideration of your goal—your influencing aims. This is the opportunity for you to make a first-cut effort at specifying what you hope to achieve through influencing decision makers. The tentative statement presumes the worthiness of your goal and is primarily designed to get you moving down the path toward approval.

Your tentative goal statement should identify your target market; that is, the specific decision maker(s) toward whom you will target your influencing energy. If you were *Esquire* magazine, for example, the target market (primary consumer) might be professional men in the middle and upper income brackets. For you, the target market might be your boss, the board of directors, or the personnel committee, for example.

Your tentative goal statement should also indicate what you hope to achieve through successful influencing. And it should contain a target date for the outcome to be accomplished. Since goals are essentially "statements of good intentions," don't be concerned now about how to measure your goal. The goal statement is crafted to articulate direction. Later, when we define objectives, we will concern ourselves with measuring accomplishment.

A tentative goal statement might read something like:

> *"I want to convince Chuck Coaley by July 15th to allocate $20,000 in next year's budget for the development of a new credit training program for the company."*

Another might read:

> *"By the end of this quarter, I would like to get Pat Rainey's approval to increase my staff by two professional people beginning in the fourth quarter of this year."*

Still another might go:

> *"No later than March 31st, I will need to get the approval of the Board of Directors to purchase three color videotape units for training in our Southeast District no later than next January."*

What is important is that the tentative goal statement be in your own words and identify what, who, and approximately when. The more clarity, the less ambiguity, in your goal statement now will help focus your energy later, since you will weave your influence strategy around the goal you ultimately select.

Now it's time to pick up a pencil and try your hand at articulating a tentative goal. In the space provided on the following page, write a first draft goal statement.

TENTATIVE GOAL STATEMENT
(First Draft)

Please review the questions in the following checklist and then check the appropriate space.

GOAL STATEMENT CHECKLIST

A. Does your statement indicate what you want to happen? ____Yes ____No

B. Does your statement identify the person(s) you will need to influence? ____Yes ____No

C. Are there approximate dates for when your influence strategy needs to be completed? ____Yes ____No

D. Is your goal achievable in the time frame identified? ____Yes ____No

E. Can your goal be done with the resources available to you? ____Yes ____No

Now, go back to questions A through C to see whether you checked any "no's." If so, you may want to reword your tentative statement. If you checked "no" for question D, you may wish to lower your sights by opting for a more realistic time frame or picking another goal. If you checked "no" for question E, you may need to marshal additional resources, or you may wish to either lower your sights or select another tentative goal. The revised goal may become a subset of your original grander goal.

Those questions about your tentative goal were designed as a quality-control procedure, to enable you to refine your goal. While it is still quite tentative, you may want to rewrite your statement in the space below if you had any reservations or answered "no" to any of the questions.

REVISED TENTATIVE GOAL STATEMENT
(Second Draft)

You may want to cycle your second draft through the Goal Statement Checklist. You have a clear statement of your tentative goal when you can answer "yes" to all the questions there.

The purpose of what you have done so far has been to surface your influencing intent and to spell out the general direction for your efforts. Every successful influencer, whether the founder of IBM or the accounting manager for XYZ Company, begins with a goal or aim. Clarity of goal, albeit tentative, is the ticket for clarifying your mission—the next step in the marketing approach to influencing.

CLARIFYING YOUR MISSION

If you want to be successful in your effort to influence decision makers, *your* goal must be in sync with the *total* organization. This may mean initially sublimating your personal or your unit viewpoint in order to take a broader, more comprehensive, organization-wide look.

"Wait a second!" you may chide, "I just want to sell my boss on adding two people. I didn't come here to contemplate the universe!"

I repeat, your success long term is absolutely dependent on aligning what *you* desire with the role and mission of the total organization. I recognize it is hard to suppress what seem like such clear, important needs of your position or your unit to favor a comprehensive organizational view. Nevertheless, being congruent with your organization's mission is key to your effectiveness as an influencer.[3]

The subtitle of this book was carefully chosen—marketing the ideas that matter! This section of the book is aimed at helping you sort out the "that matter" part. It may initially feel like a needless diversion along your route to victory. You will discover, however, that where you are about to go is *the* most important leg of your journey.

At the very core of the marketing concept is the notion of *consumer responsiveness*. A company attempting to sell a product or service wastes its money when it buys advertising that attempts to change the customers' needs. Successful companies start with what's already there—accepting the customers' needs and desires. Having done this, they use advertising to help the customers connect their needs with the company's distinctive competency (unique qualification) for meeting that need.

Enterprises go broke every day when the product or service they push fails to satisfy a need of the customer. Likewise, people in organizations go broke when their nifty idea doesn't fit the organizational mission.

> *I know a personnel manager who devised a near-perfect appraisal system for salespeople. One hitch: the company wasn't ready for the system and it never got*

---

[3]I am indebted to Bruce W. Fritch of Fritch & Company, Charlotte, North Carolina, for contributing this concept. Bruce's view is that organizational effectiveness occurs when all resources are strategically aligned with organizational mission.

*past first base. "But it's a fantastic
system," lamented the manager. Too
bad. His focus was on his goal rather
than on the organizational need.*

An employee may discover a super process for developing film
without a darkroom. But if the company is a manufacturer of
tractors...you get the picture! Your contribution—and the contribution of your unit—must be aligned with organizational mission.
Otherwise, the contribution is questionable from the start.

Let's assume an influencer in the role of training manager wanted
to get approval to begin a sales training program. The *role-* or *unit-
focused* approach might start with the manager's saying:

> *"Gee, I did sales training in my last
> company, and it worked pretty well. I
> think I'll do it here."*

or

> *"I haven't done any sales training in a
> while, I think I'll dust off the old pro-
> gram and crank it up again. Those folks
> need a good refresher."*

or

> *"I saw a terrific sales training package at
> the conference last December. It'll
> knock their socks off! I think I'll talk the
> powers-that-be into buying it."*

or

> *"I'm very familiar with the company's
> small appliance division, and I hear they
> need some sales training. I'll get started
> there and then expand it to the rest of the
> company."*

The exclusive focus of the examples above is "what do I want to
sell," rather than "what contribution can I make to helping the
organization achieve its mission?" To influence, you must be able to
discuss your goal in the context of organizational mission.

An *organization-focused* approach to sales training might sound
like this:

> *"Yes, it appears that sales training is an
> important activity for next quarter. In*

division A, for example, market share has slipped by 5 percent, according to our latest research, while competition has increased 2 percent. We know there are a variety of causes for this. One cause is that many of our salespeople lack selling skills. This is one cause that we can handle. Our company was founded on the belief that we could better serve the public if they have knowledge of what we offer. We are not able to have the kind of interface we want with the public unless our sales force can communicate what we offer effectively. Sales training is a tool for improving that customer communication."

Such a statement positions the training program within the context of corporate role (in the example above, communicating with the customer). Decision makers, conscious of this role, are readily able to see how the training manager's goal is aligned with their goal. Only if you are armed with a sense of organizational mission can you assess whether your goal will help meet the organization's priority needs.

Once you are assured there is a clear alignment between your goal and the corporate mission, you can focus energy toward helping your consumer (the decision maker) recognize how you (and your goal) are uniquely qualified to aid in achieving that mission. That, in a nutshell, is the marketing approach to influencing.

Let's explore another example to clearly differentiate the unit- or role-focused approach (the sales concept) from the organization-focused approach (the marketing concept) to influencing.

**Sales
Concept:**

"Shucks, don't talk to me about numbers. I don't understand that stuff. But, oh boy, can I build a strong team out of the accounting department! Team building is something I do really well."

"What's that? Are we going to talk about accounting in the session? No, most of my examples are about teachers. But the

*principles still apply. Now, let's talk
about what I need the participants
to do."*

**Marketing
Concept:**

*"Yes, I can do team building. But first I'd
like to interview all the people in the
accounting department who will be involved. I not only need to fully understand their functions and situation, but
their language and culture as well. I
hope to get lots of relevant examples
from my assessment to use in the
session."*

Can you sense the difference? At the core of the marketing concept,
we said earlier, is consumer responsiveness. You can be very successful
if you respond, instead of convince. Philosophically, your energy
should go toward "being with" rather than "getting from."

*Contribution to organizational mission is the keystone of your
effectiveness as an influencer.* McDonald's Corporation achieved
enormous success by aligning their contribution to the consumer's
need (desire) for food of predictable quality delivered quickly in
convenient locations. Your success happens when you align your
mission and goals with the need (desire) of your organization to
accomplish its mission in the marketplace.

Many of us spread ourselves too thin. Knowledge of organizational
mission will aid in placing energy on priorities, the ideas that matter.
Such knowledge will help to achieve a more gratifying ratio of biting to
chewing. It helps prevent our getting choked due to inadequate
capacity. With knowledge of mission, we can be efficient (doing things
right) *and* effective (doing the right things).

There are many side benefits to a constant, clear knowledge of
organizational mission. You cannot be all things to all people. You (and
your unit) alone cannot cause the organization to win at its mission. You
can only *contribute* to that win. Knowledge of mission enables you to
accurately carve out your distinctive competency, your unique
contribution.

Before proceeding further, jot down in the space on the following
page your initial thoughts on a mission statement for your unit. You will
have an opportunity shortly to revise and refine these initial thoughts.

UNIT MISSION STATEMENT

The mission of my unit is:

THE RELATIONSHIP OF POWER
TO CONTRIBUTION

In chapter 1, we briefly examined power as a key part of the marketing concept. As an influencer you will rely on the use of personal power to achieve the outcome you desire. The marketing concept is much more attuned to personal power than to role power.

Personal power—as the term is used here—is manifested first and foremost in the symbiotic energy of two or more people. It is *always* focused in a particular direction. If unfocused, it is not power. In its ideal form, it is balanced, pure, and appropriate. It is never perceived as obtrusive or oppressive. By the same token, it is not viewed as being right or wrong, good or bad, perfect or imperfect. It is more likely characterized as "feeling right," or "legitimate," or it is not even noticed at all, save its effect. There is only the sensation of its existence as a kind of centeredness which inspires confidence and trust.

It is the *direction* and *flow* of our personal power, when matched with the inevitable change of direction and flow within an organization, that establishes the alliedness or "hand and glove" impact of the effective influencer. Effectiveness emerges from the profound mutuality of purpose between one's function and the interests of key decision makers. In this way, one's personal power is focused, but it is focused in a subtle, quiet way rather than in a controlling manner. When projected at the right pace, it feels *in sync*.

In an Eastern sense, you exercise personal power when you recognize the flow of a compatible energy field and then merge with that flow. You do this by including yourself in the flow, combining the flow with your mission, which should characteristically coincide with the organization's mission.

When you look at the other side—the failure to use personal power—you see how resistance is created in others. If the person or group you are trying to influence resists a particular direction or flow of energy, you are probably not using personal power appropriately and, in an Eastern sense, are "pushing the river."

I have pushed many rivers myself, foaming some and overflowing the banks of others. I repeat, effectiveness lies in the direction of the river. One uses the energy of the river, views oneself as smaller than it, and allies oneself with its purpose.

The ease of allying yourself with change comes with your acceptance of the inevitability of change—its greater size than you—and the relaxed state you assume once having surrendered to it. Allying yourself with change causes you to create much less resistance than if you worked hard and diligently and otherwise sought to convince.

Fundamentally, an influencer is a facilitator in the purest sense of the word. A facilitator does not impede, obtrude, or create consternation. A facilitator does, however, alter direction—adjusting it, modifying it, while not disrupting the energy which is present.

One analogy that may be helpful is that role power is like electricity, personal power is like having the right appliance. You are better off seeking the right appliance than pursuing greater voltage. Part of the work of influencing is to use energy in an ecological or balanced sense. Role power has the potential of being abusive and excessive. Personal power, used appropriately, is so in tune ecologically, so unified with the persons and the organizational setting to be influenced, that, as events are changed, the presence of power remains unnoticed.

ONLY CONNECT.

—*E.M. Forster*
Howard's End

FINDING THE RIGHT COURSE

The analogy of flowing with the river is a useful one in getting a sense of alignment. Before we can "get in the flow" we must first detect the course of the river and the direction of its movement. In our organizational life, when we are oblivious to direction, we pursue film development in a tractor factory.

Take a few minutes and consider your organization's role and mission. For what reason does it attempt to exchange in the marketplace? If you asked that question of your organization's consumers, what would they say?

"I know our organization must have a role and mission," you may say, "but I've never seen it." Sometimes organizations publish and distribute their mission statements. Sometimes they do not. Written or not, a mission statement does exist, even though it may be secreted in the vision of those charged with running the organization. While there may be differences among their views, there is enough consensus for movement.

If the mission is not known to you, pursue the question with your co-workers and superiors. Look at the language in the annual report. Notice the messages in statements made by executives to employees, to stockholders, to the public.

Keep in mind that statements like "to achieve a significant return on shareholders' equity," or words to that effect, are *not* statements of mission. They point to ways to keep score, to *measure* role performance. A statement of role and mission addresses *why* the organization exists in the marketplace—*who* it is (identity) and/or *who* it hopes to be (vision).

The role and mission of Lockheed Aircraft Corporation was at one time:

1. To be the major company satisfying in the highest technical sense the national security needs of the U.S. and its allies in space, air, land, and sea.
2. To employ technical resources in meeting the nondefense needs of governments and the requirements of commercial markets.[4]

Notice the focus on consumer needs? See how easily you could hold up any corporate activity and use the mission statement to check its appropriateness? With a knowledge of corporate mission, any func-

---

[4]George A. Steiner, *Top Management Planning* (New York: Macmillan, 1969), p. 6.

tional unit in Lockheed could attest to how it contributed to "satisfying...security needs" and "meeting...nondefense needs."

Having plugged into organizational role and mission, you will be able to inspect your unit's role and mission, and then your own. The objective is to check for alignment. Is your mission following the direction and flow of the "organizational river"?

I believe it is extremely important to draft your own statement of the role and mission of your unit before proceeding to form an influence strategy. You do not want to be a "buggy whip" influencer. Even if your buggy whip happens to be the best around, it is for naught if your consumer prefers an automobile. A modern day analogy might be, "You can have the neatest spaceship in the world, but it doesn't matter a damn if nobody wants to go to the moon."

"I already know what my unit's role is, and I'm convinced it is aligned," you may be thinking. OK, that's great! You are ahead of the game. Going through the exercise might still be helpful, though. If nothing else, it will enable you to update or confirm the legitimacy of your work efforts.

Get ready to jot down mission statements in the next few pages. If you are not sure how to begin, the following model may assist.

When I began writing this book and I was clarifying my mission, I wrote:

> *My mission in writing this book is:*
> - *To speak to staff people in organizations.*
> - *To help readers become more effective in carrying out their roles.*
> - *To aid readers in learning marketing principles for influencing decision makers.*
> - *To make a contribution to employee competency and to organizational effectiveness.*

That list is the original, uncut, unedited statement of my mission. You can see how random and scattered my thoughts were. Yours may be equally disjointed at this stage. That's fine. The goal is not finished copy, the goal is to begin movement.

Now, in the space provided on the next page, quickly jot down several mission statements for *your* unit. (Refer to your initial thoughts on a mission statement.)

UNIT MISSION STATEMENTS

One of the best ways to clarify mission is to identify outcomes that signify the mission was accomplished. Prepare to specify how you will know whether you achieved your mission. You will articulate actions or results which provide verification that your mission was carried out.

For this book, my list of actions or results which would signify "mission accomplished" was:

- *The reader will be able to discuss unit needs and individual role needs within the context of the organization's mission.*
- *The reader will have a fuller grasp of the total needs of the organization.*
- *The reader will be more capable of discussing the value system of the organization.*
- *The reader will be more realistic and selective in his or her aspirations to contribute to organizational mission.*
- *The reader will display more competence in presenting his or her unit's needs.*

You can see, I was fairly uninhibited.

In the space below, write the actions or results which will evidence accomplishment of your unit's mission.

EVIDENCE OF UNIT MISSION ACCOMPLISHMENT

At this point, you have *not* settled on a mission statement. You simply put the mission issues on the page. Now you must go back and summarize these issues into a role and mission statement. Look at what you've written above. Your final mission statement will no doubt repeat some of the same words. Your ultimate statement is one you can state "from the podium" in all sincerity!

For example, my final mission statement read:

> *My purpose in writing this book is to contribute to organizations through helping professionals function more effectively in carrying out their roles. This will be done by:*
>
> - *Aiding readers in aligning their role and mission with the organization's mission.*
> - *Assisting readers to work with more realism.*
> - *Aiding readers to respond to true organizational needs.*

- *Helping readers understand and appreciate the value system of their organization.*
- *Facilitating readers' gaining more competence in presenting solutions to priority needs.*

In the space below, write the mission of your unit.

FINAL UNIT MISSION STATEMENT

The time has come to do a quality-control check on your mission statement. The questions below may assist.

MISSION STATEMENT QUALITY-CONTROL CHECKLIST

1. Is your statement understandable to all involved in accomplishing the mission? ____Yes ____No

2. Is it aligned clearly with the organization's role and mission? ____Yes ____No

3. Does it identify your unit's reason for existence, its unique contribution? ____Yes ____No

4. Does it state a contribution which is reasonable to accomplish? ____Yes ____No

5. Would your boss, the president, and the senior executives agree with a "yes" in questions 1 through 4? ____Yes ____No

If you answered "yes" to all five questions, you are ready to proceed further. If there are "no's," you either need to narrow or clarify the mission statement or check to ensure agreement among those with greater authority in the organization (or both).

"What about *my* role?" you may question, "I'd like this to be a bit more personal." Just as your unit must be aligned, so must your individual role. Only then will your personal contribution to the organization be appropriate. If you are unwilling to contribute to your unit's role, you need a new unit!

In the space below, write a statement of your role. Make certain it meshes with your unit's mission.

INDIVIDUAL ROLE STATEMENT

Now, do a quality-control check, using the same five questions you used on your unit's mission statement. These help you get in the flow, and not waste energy or increase your frustration by "pushing the river."

One's contribution in an organization manifests through a unit or personal role. Success as an influencer is tied to contribution via a role which is aligned with organizational purpose or mission. Only with this orientation can your individual and unit goals, perspectives, and tasks be legitimate and therefore "purchasable" by decision makers. Such alignment will enable you and your unit to allocate energy, time, and resources appropriately and accurately.

Alignment is a perpetual process. Knowing that alignment is your secret to long-term success as an influencer provides the impetus for realignment each time you get off course. It is easy to get knocked off course—feelings of inadequate appreciation are a common symptom of nonalignment. The challenge is to realign.

DETERMINING YOUR FINAL GOAL

You began the goal-setting phase with a specific aim or outcome in mind. By stopping to examine role and mission, you are now in a better position to determine the legitimacy (and, thus, the marketability) of your desired outcome. I don't want you slaving away on an ad campaign for a dog food that dogs won't eat. Your work stands the greatest chance of contributing to organizational mission when it is aligned with that mission and consistent with your unit's role. Don't be the film-processing inventor in a tractor factory—an extreme example to be sure, but one worth keeping in mind.

Being mission-oriented, we seek a course along which to proceed in carrying out that mission. The course along which the organization is currently proceeding is the organization's present *strategy*—much like the river, or a path to an ultimate destination. A strategy (or course) is the manner in which the organization needs to be perceived by consumers in order to carry out the mission. McDonald's *mission*, for example, might be to satisfy the convenience food desires of today's fast-paced, time-conscious consumers. If it does this well, it will "win" financially by providing franchise owners and stockholders a healthy return on their monetary investment in McDonald's.

McDonald's sells fast foods. But simply opening a store and offering a good product are not sufficient. Since other companies are aggressively competing for the customer's fast-food dollar, McDonald's must create a perception in the minds of consumers that McDonald's can meet their fast-food needs and desires better than any other company. The perception McDonald's selects to communicate is a part of its *strategy*, its course to mission accomplishment. The tools, ads, techniques, etc. used to carry out the strategy are called *tactics*.

Armed with knowledge of the organization's mission, you can then take *actions* to contribute, to move along that course. In business (and the military), we call such actions tactics. Tactics encompass those methods we adopt, steps we take, tools we use, and messages we send which help us stay aligned with the course or strategy. The strategy manifests itself in a series of tactics.

Let's examine another example of the distinction between strategy and tactics. The strategy of organization XYZ might be "to position our company so that it is perceived as the friendliest in the marketplace." Two tactics aligned with that strategy might be: (1) sufficient staffing in customer contact areas to ensure contacts with customers are not abrupt, and (2) a training program in listening skills and effective communication.

Now, return to your tentative goal statement (page 15) and read what you wrote there. My prediction is that it's more a statement of a tactic or activity than a strategy-level goal. All the examples given in that section were tactical aims—to add staff, to increase budget, to start a new program, and so forth. That's OK. Your tentative goal statement is important, and you will probably incorporate it into your influencing plan later. At this juncture, however, it is important to do a quality-control check on your goal statement by looking at a broader level—the level of mission and strategy.

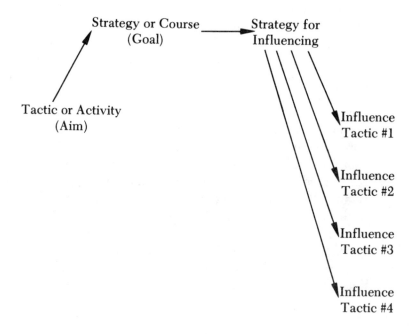

Your buyer will be more interested in a particular tactical aim if it is in the context of a unit or individual strategy for contribution to corporate mission. Therefore, it is imperative you begin the next phase (assessment) with a goal at the strategy level in hand. Adding staff, increasing budget, beginning a new program, and so on, may be useful tactics for achieving your strategy-level goal.

Take a look at figure 2, which lists a sample corporate mission statement and three corresponding corporate strategies. Beside each corporate strategy is the corresponding strategy-level goal for the human resource development unit and two tactics for each strategy. When you have a sense of how all these elements interact, you will be ready to upgrade your goal statement if necessary.

Notice that each HRD strategy statement in figure 2 has been elevated above the program or tactic level and tied inextricably to organization-wide mission. Strategic Goal #1 (aligned with Corporate Strategy A) speaks to competency improvement, not a training program. Goal #2 (aligned with Corporate Strategy B) focuses on access to job openings to reduce turnover, not a job posting program. Actions similar to those listed in the tactics column—a training program, team building, job posting—may ultimately be part of your tactical plan. Your initial aim (page 16) may likewise be part of that plan.

Having reviewed your revised goal, write your final goal statement in the space below. Make sure there is an obvious trail from your individual role through your unit's mission back to corporate mission. The Goal Statement Checklist (page 15) should be used once more. The aim here is to sharpen the final goal statement.

FINAL GOAL STATEMENT

Figure 2. Sample Strategies, Goals, and Tactics

MISSION: XYZ Company is to meet the commercial banking needs of small businesses (less than $10 million annual sales) in the northwest Wyoming area by providing quality, customized financial services and products at a fair price.

CORPORATE STRATEGIES	HRD UNIT STRATEGIC GOALS	HRD UNIT TACTICS
A. To be perceived by small business managers as having the most service-minded commercial bankers in northwest Wyoming.	1. To increase the sales competence in Division A so that market share can be improved by the end of the third quarter.	• Implement a new sales training program. • Improve the selection standards for salespeople.
B. To be perceived by the marketplace as a highly efficient, well-organized bank which is responsive to changing customer needs.	2. To decrease the conflict over accountability between Departments A and B so that the productivity of the two units can be enhanced and duplication of effort can be decreased.	• Conduct a team building session with Departments A and B. • Replace the supervisor of Department A and reprimand the supervisor of Department B.
C. To be perceived by the northwest Wyoming area as an employer that is enlightened in its approach to people-management.	3. To increase internal access to manager-level job openings so as to improve job-person match, decrease recruiting costs, and improve negative turnover among managers.	• Institute a job posting program for manager-level job openings. • Implement a human resource planning meeting quarterly for senior managers to review manager openings.

That statement you just penned will be the foundation of your new platform for influencing. If you are satisfied with what you have and are confident that it "meets the test," you are ready to proceed to assessment. In the next phase, you will further test your goal against the realities of your marketplace. And you will gather the detailed data needed to ultimately assemble your overall influencing plan.

In • flu • ence (in'floo-
ens), *n.*, *v.*, -enc • ing.

1. the process or action of producing effects on others by indirect or intangible

PART II

THE ASSESSMENT PHASE

For several years, Mary Smith and her husband, Bob, had enjoyed having friends over for dinner. While doing a year's graduate study in Italy, Mary had learned to make superb pizza. Bob prided himself on having an enormous knowledge of wines. After Mary's high school teaching position was cut during a budget squeeze, she and Bob decided to put their savings into a classy wine and pizza shop. Mary could supervise the cooking; Bob could buy the wine and handle the business management while continuing on a moderately demanding job as an electrical engineer.

They leased space in a new inner-city shopping mall and began their new career as restaurateurs. Within six months, they were out of business! Mary had learned she lacked the patience, skill, and desire to supervise people; Bob had been unable to keep up with the continuous paperwork. Even worse, the mall mainly generated lunch traffic; less than 25 percent of the business came from dinner customers. The waiting time for their speciality, made-to-order pizza, precluded the rapid customer turnaround required to capitalize on the lunch business. They went into bankruptcy, bitterly resigned, exhausted.

This sort of business story occurs all the time in our society. With minor variations, it is the tale of many in the business of influencing others within an organization. We presume that if we have inspired vision and intelligence, we will most likely succeed. When we fail, we scratch our heads and mutter, "How can a person with my brains continue to make the same errors? Nobody tries harder!"

Bob and Mary had lots of inspiration! They were also bright people. They failed, however, to assess their consumers, their marketplace, and themselves.

To simply enter the marketplace with talent and high hopes can be foolhardy. But we have all done a "Mary and Bob Smith" from time to time—leaping headlong into some activity without patiently thinking through the relevant variables. Our eagerness short-circuits our excellence. We fail to do the front-end analysis on which effective influencing depends.

The assessment phase in our influencing model is analogous to market research and analysis. The market researcher diagnoses the buyer or consumer (in your case, that's the decision makers), the marketplace (that's the organization), and the capabilities of the seller or promoter (that's you!).

Before going forward, I strongly recommend you get a package of 3″ x 5″ index cards. In the assessment phase, you will be recording and examining facts which will be consolidated to form conclusions. (We will later be referring to individual facts or pieces of evidence as *data elements*, and conclusions drawn from a number of data elements as *data conclusions*.) There will be times throughout the assessment phase when you will be asked to write your conclusions on cards. You may want to use a different colored set for each of the next three chapters. This will be a major aid at the end of this phase in coupling, consolidating, and synthesizing conclusions in order to derive priority problems and opportunities for constructing your strategy for influencing decision makers.

The assessment phase of the marketing framework for influencing contains four steps, pictured on the next page. I have included the preceding phase to help you keep track of where you are. The first three steps require focusing your assessment on a particular target— the decision makers, the organization, and you. The fourth step in the assessment phase, Step 7, involves identifying problems and opportunities, from which you plan your strategy and select appropriate influencing tactics.

PRELUDE TO ASSESSMENT

Before delving into understanding your buyer, marketplace, and you, it is important to take stock of your present resources. This will enable you to supplement insufficient resources and optimize those you have. The inventory will be a helpful backdrop for proceeding with your market research.

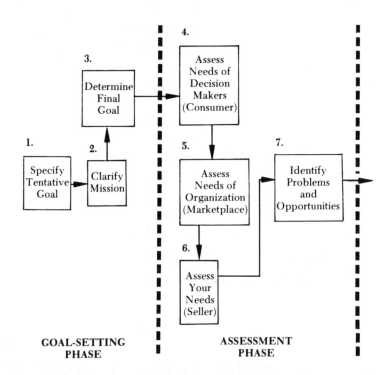

GOAL-SETTING PHASE

1. Specify Tentative Goal
2. Clarify Mission
3. Determine Final Goal

ASSESSMENT PHASE

4. Assess Needs of Decision Makers (Consumer)
5. Assess Needs of Organization (Marketplace)
6. Assess Your Needs (Seller)
7. Identify Problems and Opportunities

A resource inventory does not mean counting the paper clips and Scotch tape! It does mean active acknowledgement of people, materials, or systems currently within reach which may need to be deployed in influencing decision makers. They are the "liquid assets" at your disposal. Your inventory may surface available resources you might have overlooked without a deliberate audit.

People Resources

Here you will simply list the people who can assist you in influencing. Later, you may want to develop a plan for soliciting their aid. Sit back and take a few minutes to examine the "who's" you may want to seek. The list below offers cues to trigger names for you.

PEOPLE RESOURCES TRIGGER WORDS

1. your staff
2. your best friend
3. maitre d'
4. janitor
5. lawyer
6. print shop workers
7. decision maker's spouse
8. decision maker's best friend

9. accountant
10. minister
11. top customers
12. board members
13. secretaries
14. hairdresser
15. stock broker
16. outside salespeople
17. therapist
18. chauffeur
19. tailor
20. consultants

Record your list below. Listing people does not mean you will ask their help, only that they are there.

POTENTIAL PEOPLE RESOURCES

Another form of people resources involves the capabilities of your staff (if you have a staff) or co-workers. On the next page, make a list of the key players and the special skills they possess. This might read something like:

> *Edsel Joiner has the ability to quickly see the big picture.*
>
> *Lois Meeks has talents for writing in crisp, results-oriented language.*

*Patsy Bost has a very creative mind and
is great at generating ideas.*

You may require more space than is allotted below. Use additional sheets of paper if necessary.

UNIQUE SKILLS OF YOUR STAFF AND CO-WORKERS

Name   **Special Abilities**

Systems Resources

The processes or systems you employ to get work accomplished can also aid you in carrying out an influence strategy. These might include a well-organized filing system, persistent use of a daily "to do" list, a process for keeping co-workers informed, a budgeting system, an effective management-by-objectives system, or an efficient management information system. All these may be helpful.

List below the systems available within your arsenal of resources.

SYSTEMS RESOURCES

Material Resources

The last category in your brief resume of resources is physical or material aids. Consider these tangible items which may have special use in influencing. The cuing list below may assist you.

MATERIAL RESOURCES TRIGGER WORDS

1. a photocopy machine
2. a comprehensive library
3. subscriptions to many journals
4. a computer
5. a conference room
6. art supplies
7. a club membership
8. a flight guide
9. comfortable chairs
10. good whiskey
11. a programmable calculator
12. a company car

In the space below, write the special material resources which may aid you later in influencing decision makers.

MATERIAL RESOURCES

You will find that cataloguing resources will make remembering them later much more likely. If other resources occur to you, be sure to record them for referral.

With resource resume in hand, you are now ready to take Step 4—assessing decision makers—on your trail to successful influencing. You will call on your resource resume repeatedly throughout the remainder of this book.

3

ASSESSING THE DECISION MAKER, YOUR CONSUMER

Great minds have purpose,
others have wishes.

—Washington Irving

A well-known *Fortune* 500 company was losing market share for one of the major products in its paper products division—toilet paper. Different approaches to reverse the trend had been tried with little success. The marketing director concluded she needed better research data on the consumer. The company's continually missing the mark with its advertising had to be related to the data base on which the ad campaigns were founded.

The market research unit turned to a consumer psychologist to enrich the data they had already collected and, perhaps, to provide a fresh perspective. The psychologist returned with the finding that toilet paper buyers use toilet paper in one of two ways: they fold it or they wad it. Moreover, the wadder consumes far more toilet paper than the folder.

The consumer psychologist also determined that the personality makeup of the wadder was considerably different from the profile of the folder. Armed with the insights gained from an assessment of the decision maker in the marketplace, the company set about restructuring its marketing strategy, product line, packaging, advertising, and sales tactics to appeal primarily to the personality of the wadder. The campaign was successful and the toilet paper division dramatically increased its share of the market.

This story points to the critical importance of conducting a careful assessment of the potential consumer. For the influencer, that consumer is the person or persons who make decisions about the suitability of the influencer's proposal. Among the variables affecting consumer decisions is the psychological makeup of the consumer.

We have all learned psychology at various "mothers' knees." Some of us have acquired our insight through our own lives, going through the school of hard knocks. Others have embellished on that knowledge through academic courses related to human behavior. What follows is a brief review of some of the key points in understanding human (in this case, decision makers') behavior.

At first blush, this chapter may seem strangely organized, repeatedly passing over the same ground. Assessing decision makers is like peeling an onion. Each layer may appear quite similar to the last, but continuous removal of layers takes you closer to the core. By the end of the chapter, after several cycles of applying the concepts presented, you will have a much more accurate assessment than your initial attempts could have produced. The goal here is not to become an instant shrink. Psychological assessment is a tool for understanding, so that your influence strategy is in accord with the uniqueness of your decision makers.

We begin our journey through consumer psychology by reviewing one view of how personality is developed in human beings.

THE FOUNDATIONS OF CONSUMER PSYCHOLOGY

When a baby is born, it initially perceives the world with a sense of omnipotence. It has complete control over its environment, at least from its perspective. When the baby cries or whimpers, things seem to magically happen. Diapers get changed. Toys get rattled. The baby gets rocked, cuddled, turned, burped, or a nipple is placed in its mouth. Like magic! With a simple whimper, all things are at the baby's beck and call.

Some months after the baby's birth, it discovers that it is not its personal omnipotence that creates such rapid response, but rather something outside itself called a mommy or daddy. The baby quickly realizes that it is to a large degree at the beck and call of someone else. Through experimentation with behavior, the baby quickly begins to figure out what it takes to control these external forces. This figuring-out process begins the basis for the personality makeup or psychological *needs* structure of the individual.

Needs are synonymous with *motives* or *drives*, depending on which psychology textbook you read. Needs are the major energy source for individual actions, and one's needs are shaped by a variety of forces. First are the kinds of role models the child has growing up. Parents, teachers, and other significant people who exert influence over the child tend to communicate that they value certain behaviors more than others. Likewise, the kind of actions on a child's part that are rewarded or reinforced by people of influence tend to shape the behavior of the child.

A few examples may be helpful. I was raised in an environment in which order and neatness were valued. Not only were my parents orderly, neat people, but when I kept my room cleaned up, my toys put away, my shirt tucked in, my hair combed, my face washed, and my bed made, good things happened. When I failed to do these things, I often experienced the disapproval, if not the wrath, of my parents.

With reinforcement plus role models, I developed a relatively strong need for neatness and order. Now, I find myself uncomfortable in settings in which things are not in order and neat. I constantly want to straighten my business partner's desk. If I enter a room in which a picture is hanging crooked, I am compelled to go forward and straighten it. My need for order is tightly woven into my personality framework, and if you are going to influence me, your approach must have a fair amount of order to it if you want me to respond favorably.

There are other needs, values, or motives. Some of us have a high need to achieve. We learn early on that winning, being the best, measuring up, and doing things better than others give us a sense of satisfaction. No doubt, we grew up in settings where achievement was valued, recognized, and acknowledged, or we had parents who were themselves achievers.

I have a friend who, from an early age, was told to expect the best, demand the best, be the best. When she came home with a high mark on an exam, the first question out of her mother's mouth was, "Did anyone else score higher?" When she went out for the girls' track team in high school, her dad told her, "If you're going to the trouble to go out for track, you might as well set a school record that will stand for a while." She has gone through life ardently pursuing achievement.

I have another friend who has a high need to be liked. Not only did he grow up in a warm, conflict-free environment, but his parents stressed the importance of being liked, being popular, and being recognized by others. As an adult, he devotes an inordinate amount of energy to doing things for others and engaging in activities that will gain him the recognition and acceptance of others.

There are people who have a high psychological need for control. Growing up in home environments where errors and mistakes were viewed with disdain, they learned that if they controlled their environments to the maximum degree possible—situations, people, themselves—there would be less chance for them to blunder and look foolish. They are most comfortable with things they can place in neatly labeled boxes—right or wrong, black or white, legal or illegal. The gray, ambiguous aspects of life are frustrating to them, because they defy control. Some carry this need for control to its greatest extreme— a need to be perfect. They avoid error constantly, often becoming sticklers for details, dotting every *i*, crossing all the *t*'s.

THE NEEDS OF THE DECISION MAKERS

You can, no doubt, see how awareness of consumers' needs or motives could be useful in planning an influence strategy. If a decision maker in your organization has a high need to achieve, positioning your idea as a way for him or her to win, accomplish a goal, "be the best," or experience a challenge could cause it to be more readily accepted. If your decision maker has a high need for approval, affiliation, or recognition, your proposal could be positioned to bring the decision maker kudos from others. On and on—knowledge of motives or needs serves you well in planning your influencing approach.

If your decision maker has a high need for control, for example, your proposal should have a clear-cut way for the decision maker to provide input and make modifications. High-control individuals need to feel like they can modify things and ideas to suit their comfort zone. If control needs are in the perfectionistic range, your proposal needs to be precise down to the nitpickiest detail. Be prepared for the high-control decision maker to scrutinize every angle in search of flaws. Don't be alarmed if a tiny error is noted and corrected. What is important is that errors are absent from the essential substance of your proposal.

There is a host of needs that may direct people's actions. Some of the examples listed below may be useful in your comprehensive assessment of the needs of key decision makers to be involved in achieving your goal.

EXAMPLES OF PSYCHOLOGICAL NEEDS

1. Maintaining a power base within the organization.
2. Personal growth and competence.
3. Stability, security, and predictability.
4. Affiliation and acceptance within a group.
5. A need to help others.
6. Making a good impression on others.
7. Being viewed as fair and considerate.

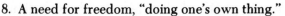

8. A need for freedom, "doing one's own thing."
9. Being viewed as creative or innovative.
10. A need for change, diversity, and new experiences.
11. A need for control or dominance.
12. Being liked or recognized by others.
13. Being the best, accomplishing a challenging goal, winning.
14. Being seen by others as intelligent or always right.

At this point, you may be saying, "OK, that makes sense, but I'm no shrink. How can I accurately diagnose the psychological needs of the people I must influence?" Be patient! We will shortly explore more concepts and techniques which will increase your accuracy.

Before proceeding, however, think of your final goal statement and identify the person or persons you need to influence. Write their names and titles (e.g., chief executive, senior production manager, personnel director) in the space below.

KEY DECISION MAKERS

Name of Decision Maker   **Title**

Now, select one of the people identified above, preferably the one you know best. If you only listed one person, obviously, that is the person you will assess. Think about how that person acts at work. What does he or she emphasize? What things appear to be most important to him or her?

In the space below, examine that person's actions and *hypothesize* about his or her top psychological needs or motives. Refer to the preceding list of needs for assistance.

NEEDS HYPOTHESES

Name	Actions (Data Elements)	Possible Needs (Conclusions)

You will do this same activity again later in this chapter, after examining additional perspectives for decision maker assessment. Each time your conclusions will be more definite.

NEEDS, CHOICES, AND ACTIONS

We have examined the concept of needs as a method of assessing decision makers. Needs are the basis for behavior. While this is not a textbook on psychology, a deeper understanding of consumer psychology can be an important dimension to developing a marketing plan for influencing decision makers in your organization. The concepts to follow are aimed at making your psychological needs assessment much more accurate and comprehensive.

There are many theories of personality and human behavior. Each has its principles as well as its proponents. The principles outlined below represent *one* way of viewing behavior, not the *only* way. Use them if they help create insight; discard them if they do not. They represent an eclectic sampling of the personality theories of many.[5]

1. *We all have a set of psychological needs or motives acquired largely through our experience with what has worked in our lives.* These needs provide much of the energy for our behavior and are principally gained through our experience with early role models and the actions that were favored by those role models.

2. *Most of us have very similar needs; we differ in the importance, priority, or weight we place on a particular need.* For instance, my *high* need to be liked might be only a moderate need of yours. Your high need to achieve might be a low need of mine. We both have needs to achieve and to be liked. We may be different in the force they play in our lives. Part of your challenge in developing an influence strategy is to assess the high-priority needs of the key decision makers.

3. *We are always engaging in some kind of behavior.* Every moment of our lives we are engaging in specific actions. If we are not behaving, we are either asleep, unconscious, or dead! Some theorists say behavior occurs during sleep and unconsciousness—for our purposes, it doesn't matter.

4. *We generally have a choice as to how we will behave or act.* That is, at any given moment, a person has more than one option for how to behave, to act. Sometimes these choices may seem small, but they in fact exist.

5. *The choice of behavior a person makes is the one that makes the most sense to that person at the time.* Stated differently, people never choose to engage in wrong, stupid, or ridiculous actions at the moment they make the choice. Given the individual's self-image and view of the situation at the moment, and given the fact there is a choice about which option to pursue, the individual always makes the choice that appears to be the correct one at the time.

Thus, behavior is quite self-serving. Even the mother who rushes into a burning building to rescue her child or the soldier who throws himself on a grenade in a foxhole to protect the lives of his friends is engaging in an action that is essentially self-serving. That is, it is the best decision for her or him to make *at the time.* Yes, people are altruistic; they care and have concern for others, but the primary drive for action

---

[5]I am indebted to Richard Furr, Tony Putman, and Jim Farr for adding to my understanding of human behavior. Dr. Richard M. Furr is a principal with LEAD Associates, Inc., in Charlotte, North Carolina; Dr. Anthony O. Putman is president of Descriptive Systems in Ann Arbor, Michigan; Dr. James N. Farr is president of Farr-Crookshank, Inc., in Greensboro, North Carolina.

is grounded first in its relationship to a high-priority need or value of that individual. Just moments after a particular action, the person may say, "Gee, that was stupid of me." Or, you and I may label another's behavior as wrong or stupid. *But*, at the time the person chooses a particular action, it is in his or her view the best choice.

6. *The choice of actions or behaviors is based on the high psychological needs of the person.* That is, the choice of behavior an individual makes is the one he or she thinks at the time (given his or her self-image and view of the situation) will potentially maximally satisfy a high or important need. To use my earlier story about myself, if I entered a room with a picture hanging crooked on the wall, given my high need for order, my first action or behavior would be to straighten the picture. In fact, I would feel uncomfortable in the room until the picture was level.

7. *A psychological need, no matter how high a priority it may have, is dormant until we perceive some opportunity to meet that need.* That is, any given action or behavior is perceived by a person to be maximally motivating.

A question you might ask yourself regarding your consumer (the decision maker) is: how must this person view himself or herself and the environment in order to conclude that it makes sense to do what he or she is doing? This leads to a very powerful formula first suggested to me by Tony Putman.

$$N + O = A$$

That is, the individual's *need* (N) plus a perceived *opportunity* to meet a need (O) equals *action* or behavior on the part of an individual (A). Motivation is defined as human energy directed at a goal or opportunity the individual *perceives* will meet a high-priority need.

If you have a high need or motive (achievement, recognition, control, power, whatever), even a small opportunity to meet that need will elicit a large amount of action or behavior on your part.

$$N + o = A$$

The reverse is also true. If a small need or motive is involved, even the presentation of a large opportunity to meet that need will elicit little action or behavior.

$$n + O = a$$

Your objective as an influencer is to focus on the high-priority needs or motives of the decision maker. The accuracy of needs identification is enhanced by observing the actions decision makers choose in a given situation and hypothesizing what high need precipitated a certain action. If you observed me straighten a crooked picture when I walked into your office, you might hypothesize that I was acting or behaving to satisfy a high need for order.

Let's suppose I have a proposal to present to the company president for final approval. The proposal is well-planned and well-organized, grounded in corporate mission, complete with a report of the effective changes to occur in the pilot program and an analysis of the return on investment to the company. However, the budget-cutting ax is on the upswing in my company, and the kinds of programs I am proposing have been early victims in past economic squeezes. I realize it will take more than simply articulating the proposal's merits to the company president to win approval. I also know the president has a high need to be seen as an intellectual. Positioning the proposal in a way that approval would enhance the president's self-image as a fiscally responsible intellectual increases the chance of approval. For example, the proposal might be heavily footnoted, constructed as a potential article for publication with the president listed as coauthor, and couched in language identifying it as an enlightened breakthrough.

In a nutshell, the secret is to recognize your consumer's needs and then to structure the product or idea you are trying to "sell" in such a way that the potential consumer perceives it as an opportunity to satisfy a large need.

$$N + O = A$$

You can identify some of your decision maker's high-priority needs by literally doing nothing except to watch his or her actions. Remember, the actions you observe are produced by the decision maker's needs plus the opportunity he or she uses to satisfy those needs. When repeated opportunities are used by the decision maker to satisfy personal needs, the clues become more and more obvious. The more you can "do nothing," thus not becoming a part of the situation or opportunity, the more you increase your chances of observing pure need or motive in action.

A friend of mine who is a consulting psychologist sometimes enters the office of a potential client and simply stands and "does nothing" except say good morning with a rather neutral expression. Sometimes, the potential client rushes forward to exchange hand-shakes (a need for affiliation?); others stand but remain at their desks (a need for power?). Whatever action the potential client takes, it provides the *beginning* of a diagnosis.

Think about your key decision makers. What are some actions taken in the past few months that may be linked to a high-priority need? What actions have you heard about? Jot down your thoughts in the space below. This time you may note you are able to state conclusions with more certainty.

DECISION MAKER ACTIONS AND NEEDS

Actions	Possible Needs
(Data Elements)	(Conclusions)

FEAR AND THE DECISION MAKER'S NEEDS

Another perspective on understanding psychological needs is to look at anger. Some authorities say anger, like hate, is a secondary behavior—a manifestation of the primary behavior, fear. Fear is usually the flip side of a high-priority need. For example, people who have a high need for achievement have an accompanying fear of not measuring up. People who have a high need for power have a fear of losing control. People who have a high need for approval have a fear of rejection. Often, to examine the situations in which a key decision maker manifests anger is to gain a peephole into the decision maker's strongest needs.

In the space provided below, write what you know about the areas around which the decision maker displays anger. Now, if you presumed the anger was in reality a subconscious fear that a high need was being frustrated (or under threat of being frustrated), what need might that be? Jot down your ideas in the right-hand column.

FEAR ASSESSMENT

Decision Maker	Displays Anger When...	Possible Need

ASSESSING DECISION MAKERS THROUGH POSSESSIONS

While "what you own is what you are" is admittedly an overstatement, it reflects a large measure of the conventional valuing system in our culture. That is, another way of understanding needs is to examine the possessions an individual chooses.

People often demonstrate who they are by the kind of artifacts they collect. Look around the office of a key decision maker. What memorabilia do you find? What books are there? What do individuals who display plaques, diplomas, or certificates on their walls say about themselves? What do the pictures you see on people's credenzas indicate about their lives? What kind of car does the person drive?

People who drive a Mercedes Benz (given they could afford one) communicate a different message than the individual who possesses a Saab or a Buick or a Jeep, a sports car or a station wagon. Examine the clothes the decision maker wears. Are they off the rack, custom-tailored, designer-labeled or homemade? Are the pockets or cuffs monogrammed? Begin thinking about your decision maker's possessions now. At the end of this chapter, you will have an opportunity to use this data to draw further conclusions about the decision maker's needs.

It is important to remember that any clue is virtually meaningless by itself. The fact that the decision maker always wears a white dress shirt and bow tie, or drives a Ford when she could afford a Porsche, may mean little on its own. However, as each hunch is coupled with another, individual clues begin to form a personality mosaic.

Your goal is not to become a junior psychologist overnight! You are not required to delve into decision makers' psyches, their innermost hopes and fears. Everything I've suggested about decision makers' needs is data which is already there for your review. The purpose of this chapter is to simply provide a structure for making some sense out of it.

ASSESSING DECISION MAKERS THROUGH HOBBIES

The last layer of onion to be peeled in your assessment of the needs of the key decision makers is to look at the hobbies they choose. Often, noticing how people spend their leisure time can aid in understanding needs and motives. Finding out about hobbies might add confirming, validating data to your conclusions from your assessment in other areas.

In an article in *Sky* magazine, Dr. Irwin Ross outlines some intriguing ways of viewing a person from the perspective of his or her hobbies. He organizes his observations of possible motives or needs associated with certain hobbies into eight categories: mechanical, scientific, collecting, music or literature, photography, sports, theater or movies, and painting.[6]

---

[6]Irwin Ross, "What Your Hobby Reveals," *Sky*, February 1979, pp. 24-26. The portions of Dr. Ross's article which follow have been reprinted through the courtesy of Halsey Publishing Co., publishers of Delta *Sky* magazine.

Mechanical

If an individual likes puttering around the garage, turning out furniture on a lathe, or even toying with electric trains, the person is likely to be easygoing, who can take troubles in stride. The individual takes quiet pride in accomplishments and finds pleasure in small things.

Scientific

An interest in astronomy, geography, archeology often indicates an individual who is well-adjusted, mature, with an outgoing personality. Their interests tend to be broad, and they generally would rather laugh than bicker.

Collecting

Collectors are usually intelligent people. If you belong to this group, you are apt to be inquisitive, even nosey. They have a thirst to know everything about whatever they do and the people they meet and while this may get them into awkward situations at times, they are never bored with life. They are level-headed and good conver-sationalists.

Music or Literature

Being sensitive, which members of this group are apt to be, is a mixed blessing. They are moody and easily hurt; often carried away by their feelings. They have a hard time keeping their temper and adjusting to minor irritations. One fine quality which makes life pleasant for these people is their keen sense of humor.

Photography

Like stamp collecting, photography embraces many things. The mechanics of photographic equipment, the art of taking pictures, and the science of processing the photographs. These people are less likely to be worriers than the average. They are chatty, usually good-natured, reliable, and tackle many interests with optimism and eagerness.

Sports

The person is likely to be a cheerful, sometimes careless person if they follow active outdoor sports. They thrive on competition and, for this reason, they may appear materialistic; more interested in the fight (their work or career) than the goal. They have a great deal of charm, are enterprising and courageous, and probably a lot of fun at a party.

Theater or Movies

People in this category are often withdrawn and are more interested in the world of make believe than in reality. They have a playful imagination and are romantic—even if their feet aren't always squarely on the ground. Their mind is too active to let themselves become bored.

Painting

The individual who enjoys painting is typically bright, interesting, but often moody; sudden new ideas catch fire with them but their enthusiasm is sometimes fleeting. They have a lot of energy and are fascinated by new sights and personalities, but they leap from one interest to another. This isn't due to a lack of concentration, but by a surplus of imagination, being more interested in color than facts. They often exaggerate; they are a forceful and spirited person.

Now, begin to pull together what you know and draw a tentative hypothesis. Some further research may be necessary to round out your hypothesis.

POSSESSIONS AND AVOCATIONS ASSESSMENT

Decision Maker	Revealing Possessions	Avocations or Hobbies	Possible Needs

MERGING YOUR DATA

Based on the data elements you have considered up to this point, what would you conclude to be the high-priority needs of the decision makers? For later use, put the conclusions that you list on the next page on 3″ x 5″ index cards. This will aid you in assembling all your assessment data in order to derive priority problems and opportunities for an influence strategy.

FINAL DECISION MAKER ASSESSMENT

Name   **Priority Need or Desire**

This chapter has presented a multifaceted look at decision maker needs. We explored psychological needs as the basis of understanding the values upon which decision makers base many of their actions. By examining their actions at work, their hobbies, possessions, displays of emotion, a tentative picture of the "consumer" emerges.

The approach presented here is by no means foolproof, or even scientific. Behavior is far too complex to be reduced to a few basic rules or analyzed solely through a few intuitive techniques. The logic of people (psycho-logic) is a field in which we have much to learn. However, by becoming perpetual observers of behavior, our perceptions will be more accurate and our attempts to influence will become more successful.

Having completed this part of the assessment phase, you are now ready to move to assessing the organization—your marketplace. If you feel yourself straining at the reins, relax! The marketing approach to influencing is not a shoot-from-the-hip approach. It entails great thought and comprehensive planning.

ASSESSING THE ORGANIZATION, YOUR MARKETPLACE

*...the collecting of data is a discriminating
activity, like the picking of flowers and
unlike the action of a lawnmower; and the
selection of flowers considered worth
picking, as well as their arrangement into a
bouquet, are ultimately matters of
personal taste.*

—Arthur Koestler
The Act of Creation

Once upon a time, there was a cobbler who had the well-deserved reputation of being the best shoemaker in the area. People came from far away to buy shoes from him. The demand quickly exceeded his ability to supply shoes and he asked another good cobbler to join him. Life was busy, but manageable. Communications were informal and disputes settled swiftly. Records were kept in a ledger book, supplies were readily obtained from the local tanner, and marketing was done by the word-of-mouth advertising of satisfied customers.

You may have already figured out where this story is going. Success bred success and many more cobblers were hired. Machines increased output, word-of-mouth advertising was amplified by sales-people in the field, and supplies and raw materials were purchased from various distributors all over the country. The simple ledger gave way to computers and CPA's. Communication occurred primarily through formal reporting relationships, and disputes were settled through complicated rules and procedures. The cobbler's business evolved into an "organization."

Some have characterized an organization as individual enterprise magnified to distortion. While this is admittedly a pessimistic view, it provides a perspective useful to the influencer. Getting the sense of the total organization is sort of like the doctor's forming an impression of a whole person. It requires the forest perspective rather than tree inspection.

Step 5—assessing the needs of your organization—is an integral part of your forming a plan to influence. As for Mary and Bob Smith, who misjudged the market for their pizza shop, dangers lurk for those who inaccurately read the readiness of the market to accept their goal.

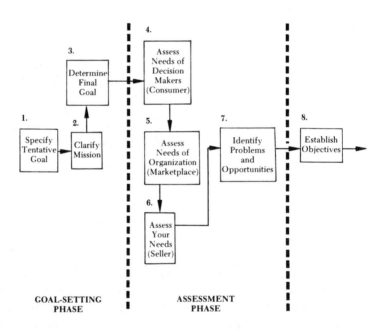

In constructing the marketing approach to influencing model, I placed exploring the needs of the key decision makers before assessment of the organization because the decision maker assessment may give you new insight into the organization. Some could argue for doing Step 5 before Step 4. You do what works for you. The point is that early in the development of your marketing plan, the needs of the organization *and* the needs of the decision makers must be considered.

The goal of this chapter is to shake up your old ways of thinking about your marketplace, to undermine your biases. I want you to have clear vision as you *see* your organization for the purpose of assessing its needs. This chapter will, I hope, aid you in gaining maximum clarity and optimum objectivity.

There are assorted ways of "seeing" organizations. Getting a "feel of the workplace," as Fritz Steele calls it, entails feeling/experiencing/sensing a work environment from a number of perspectives.[7] It is as though you had a collection of glasses, each with different colored lenses. Wearing a particular set of lenses (using a particular perspective) reveals the culture—issues, problems, and opportunities not visible with another pair. Part of the assessment process requires facility with lenses. Only by multiplying perspectives can you attain sufficient perceptual scope and depth for resolving issues related to the marketing of your goal. It helps to recognize the difference between the organization's needs and your perception of its needs.

This chapter will connect you and your skills at "seeing." Not all the lenses will be unveiled—I by no means know them all. Starting down the path of assessment, however, will begin a momentum in you, freeing you to discover which lenses you need to be useful to your purpose.

WHY ASSESS THE ORGANIZATION?

Why is this necessary? There are several reasons relevant to your success at influencing. Some are listed below. Many of these relate to the cultural values of the organization. I have left some space for you to add reasons.

REASONS FOR ASSESSMENT

1. To get a better idea about what your marketplace really wants and needs. Remember the dog food adage?
2. To more easily focus your efforts toward the area of the organization where you believe you have the greatest promise. That is, you segment your market in order to target your energy more efficiently. Remember the biting-to-chewing ratio? Market segmentation is a key dimension of success as an influencer.
3. To get more insight into the feasibility of your strategic goal as well as into the legitimacy of your contribution.
4. To sharpen the target date on your goal.

---

[7]Fritz Steele, *The Feel of the Workplace* (Reading, Mass.: Addison-Wesley, 1977).

5. To better gauge the potential receptivity to your goal. This will be very important later—as you create a marketing strategy.
6. To more accurately identify the *real* decision makers. We often learn too late in the game who is really calling the shots.
7.

8.

9.

An accurate assessment of an organization requires appropriate frameworks, models for understanding. You cannot walk into an organization and begin by saying, "Hey, I'm Studs Terkel—tell me about work." If you have models or frameworks for your assessment work, then your questions can be more focused and the discrepancy between reality and ideals can be more apparent.

You need to experience the organization in a variety of ways so that the total effect has depth and meaning. It is not just a long look—it is a measured, complete look. Carl Sagan looked at the cosmos. Edward Hall looked at proxemics. Margaret Mead looked at the Mindugomores in New Zealand. Jay Bronowski looked at science. Peter Drucker looked at the concept of the corporation.

> *Before I wore shoes, I had never known*
> *of leather. Now that I have shoes, the*
> *world is covered in leather.*

If you have a model from which to pattern your impressions, your whole perception is enriched.

GAP IDENTIFICATION

The first approach we will explore for assessing the needs of the organization is called gap identification.[8] Organizations generally

---

[8]Bruce W. Fritch has found gap identification to be an extremely useful process for assessing organizational effectiveness. His conceptual approach is described in this section.

evolve as in the cobbler's story. Often, they get bigger; then they get better. They grow faster quantitatively than qualitatively.

The cobbler had no difficulty when one person maintained the accounting system with a spindle for tickets filled out. At the end of the day, so many tickets could be checked off, "We've done these. I've delivered those. I haven't paid for this. That's Mrs. Smith—she won't pay until the end of the month, but she always pays." The system was easy to keep track of.

The *form*—that is, the process by which individual orders were kept on the spindle, checked off, entered into the ledger—was in synchronization with the *substance*, which is what was required in the situation. As the organization grew larger, the old form no longer fit the new substance. Increases in substance—in the size, character, complexity, or nature of the work—require a similar shift in the form for managing that substance. When substance and form are out of sync, gaps exist. The purpose of examining gaps is to gain greater sensitivity to the *perceived* needs of the organization versus the *actual* needs.

All organizations need certain forms in order to operate. For instance, there needs to be a system for some sort of planning. For the cobbler, that system might simply be asking himself, "What am I going to do? What materials will I need for the work I'll probably have next week?" As an organization gets larger, the complexity, design, and character of its plan—the *form* of the plan—must match the changing *substance*.

Another form all organizations need is a definition of purpose. Another is some type of organizational infrastructure—that is, the way in which people, materials, and systems operate together for the organization to achieve its purpose. Organizations need some access to their marketplace. There need to be tasks, objectives, performance standards, and so on, linked to financial objectives. There needs to be a management information system of some kind. All forms to manage substance.

When Substance Outpaces Form

A fundamental characteristic of the growth of any organism is the occurrence of gaps between what exists and what is required. For example, adolescents experience a gap between their physical development and emotional development. Much frustration and anxiety are then centered around that distortion. An example of a common organizational form-substance gap is the proliferation of hard data within the organization, on the one hand, and the organization's inability to make meaningful decisions using that data, on the other. It is far easier for a manager to get more data (via computers, research studies, reports) than it is for the members of the organization to achieve the wisdom needed to fully comprehend and rationally use the available data.

The point of all this is that a certain form is appropriate to each organization, whether it is one entrepreneur or a huge, complex corporation. Your task in assessing your organization is to determine where gaps or distortions occur. In what areas are the form which exists and the substance which is required out of sync?

The list of questions in the following checklist provides several cues to aid you in identifying areas in your organization in which the substance has outpaced the form needed to manage that substance. Examine the list and check the appropriate block for each item. For any item you give a "yes" to, rate its effectiveness in the right-hand column, with "1" being totally ineffective and "10" being extremely effective.

FORM-SUBSTANCE CHECKLIST

	Yes	No	Don't Know	Rating of Effectiveness
1. Is there a well-defined, widely communicated statement of organizational mission or purpose?	☐	☐	☐	___
2. Do employees have clear work goals (or objectives) and an effective system for their being motivated?	☐	☐	☐	___
3. Is there an organizational structure which provides for:				
a. Adequate span of control?	☐	☐	☐	___
b. Balanced allocation of resources?	☐	☐	☐	___
c. Sufficient interdependence between units?	☐	☐	☐	___

	Yes	No	Don't Know	Rating of Effectiveness

4. Are there training activities that provide employees the competencies needed for accomplishment of their work objectives? ☐ ☐ ☐ ____

5. Is there a process for ensuring the right people are in the right work roles? ☐ ☐ ☐ ____

6. Does the organization have effective ways of ensuring employees get performance feedback which:

   a. Is timely? ☐ ☐ ☐ ____

   b. Is communicated clearly? ☐ ☐ ☐ ____

   c. Is usable in improving performance? ☐ ☐ ☐ ____

7. Do employees have a way of determining the priority of their work objectives to enable them to put the greatest energy on the most important tasks? ☐ ☐ ☐ ____

8. Is there a method for communicating management information needed to achieve work objectives? ☐ ☐ ☐ ____

9. Does the organization have a process that allows employees to contribute to the development of work objectives? ☐ ☐ ☐ ____

	Yes	No	Don't Know	Rating of Effectiveness

10. Are there methods for employees to be appropriately rewarded for their contribution? ☐ ☐ ☐ ___

11. Do employees have the tools and aids they need to perform their work? ☐ ☐ ☐ ___

12. Is there a process that ensures employees have the freedom they need to perform their work effectively? ☐ ☐ ☐ ___

13. Are job descriptions:

   a. Existent? ☐ ☐ ☐ ___

   b. Up to date? ☐ ☐ ☐ ___

   c. Communicated to employees? ☐ ☐ ☐ ___

   d. Used by manager *and* employee? ☐ ☐ ☐ ___

14. In the space below, add your own areas for consideration.

_____ ☐ ☐ ☐ ___

_____ ☐ ☐ ☐ ___

_____ ☐ ☐ ☐ ___

_____ ☐ ☐ ☐ ___

_____ ☐ ☐ ☐ ___

The goal of the Form-Substance Checklist is to identify gaps. All "no's" and any "yes's" rated less than 10 point to potential gaps between what is and what should be. The "don't know's" signify areas you need to explore more fully, until you are satisfied the information either does not exist or you cannot gain access to it.

Bruce Fritch states that one of the important means of assessing organizations through gap identification is to look at form-substance dichotomies. One type of form-substance dichotomy is the variance between language used and actions employed. An example of this type of dichotomy is the organization that claims commitment to affirmative action practices but when reality is examined, not only is there racial imbalance, but no consequences for managers who perform well or poorly in affirmative action efforts.

The disparity between form and substance that occurs when the organization's needs outpace the means to meet those needs might be pictured as in figure 3. The farther apart the circles are (that is, the wider the gap), the greater the anxiety, frustration, and discord are likely to be within the organization. If your goal can be positioned as a way to reduce the gap (thus diminishing the discord), it will have a greater chance of being approved. Most decision makers gravitate toward solutions that diminish corporate pain, particularly when pain is related to low productivity or high cost.

Figure 3. Form-Substance Disparity

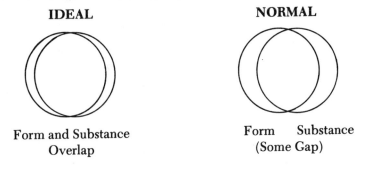

IDEAL

Form and Substance
Overlap

NORMAL

Form   Substance
(Some Gap)

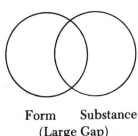

MAJOR PROBLEMS

Form   Substance
(Large Gap)

When Form Outpaces Substance

Another way form and substance get out of sync is when people in the organization have one foot so planted in the outside world that they uncritically embrace the latest bell and whistle. The danger is the bells and whistles have a way of constantly pressuring the organization to keep up with the Joneses, whether it fits what the organization requires or not. The president of a company with an overly aggressive data processing manager might lament, "We have a Rolls Royce computer and we're still just a Ford."

There is merit, of course, in an organization's staying up with or leading its competitors. Acquiring or creating a new form well ahead of what the organization actually requires can be an effective way of encouraging growth and planning for advancement. The problem comes when the gap becomes so wide that it creates undue anxiety and needless disruption.

Think of forms (systems, tools, equipment, processes, and so on) in your organization that you think far exceed what is actually required (or will be required in the near future). Jot down your thoughts below.

FORMS THAT OUTPACE SUBSTANCE

Now, complete the sentences in the Form-Substance Review.

FORM-SUBSTANCE REVIEW

The last big fad in my organization was (MBO, TA, quality circles, zero-base budgeting, data processing, job enrichment, human resource accounting, you name it):

The success of the item I mentioned above has been:

The approximate cost has been:

Other fads in my organization or industry are:

Understanding how your organization tends to get form and substance out of whack can aid in learning the organizational culture. Likewise your later strategy can both accommodate the way things are (starting where the organization is) while helping to narrow the gap.

You can identify gaps by staying attuned to the top concerns among key decision makers. Anticipate the emphasis. Will there be a short-term shift in objectives, markets, products, services, or people?

Such short-term shifts are often due to the pinches created by gaps between what is and what needs to be. As these concerns relate to your goal, ask yourself, "Why should a decision maker do something different? Why should my idea, project, or request be approved?"

Keep in mind that decisions about your goal will be business decisions and, as such, will reflect the value system of the decision makers and the organization. Decision makers do not don a special staff hat when they consider a staff proposal. I repeat, decision makers do *not* don a special staff hat when they consider a staff proposal. The proposal is viewed in the same light as any other important business decision to be made.

INSPECTING WHAT'S TO COME

Another perspective helpful in your comprehensive assessment of the organization is to consider where the organization hopes to be in the future. Armed with this perspective, you may effectively position your proposal by billing it as a way for the organization to move in the direction it seeks to go. This is, in part, what major companies do through their ad campaigns. "Coke adds life." "You deserve a break today." "Join the Pepsi generation." "Come to Marlboro Country." "We are driven." "Wouldn't you like to be a Pepper too?" And so on.

Think of what the next two years hold for your organization. What are the chances there will be a major change in any of the areas listed below? Check the appropriate box for each item.

LONG-TERM ASSESSMENT EXERCISE

	Small Chance	Some Chance	Good Chance	I Need To Find Out
• Organization structure	☐	☐	☐	☐
• Organization's perception of its purpose or mission	☐	☐	☐	☐

	Small Chance	Some Chance	Good Chance	I Need To Find Out
• Products or services that the organization provides to its customers	☐	☐	☐	☐
• Markets or areas in which the organization operates	☐	☐	☐	☐
• Legal and regulatory environment	☐	☐	☐	☐
• Customers' perception of the organization	☐	☐	☐	☐
• People who are key decision makers in the organization	☐	☐	☐	☐

Which changes in the list above will logically require a response from you for that change to be implemented effectively? Jot your thoughts in the space below.

MY ROLE IN LONG-TERM CHANGES

An acquaintance of mine had an outstanding training proposal shot down in the boardroom because he failed to assess that the company was on the verge of reorganization. He could have easily had access to the information about the impending reorganization if he had pursued it. But his proposal was couched in terms of the existing organization, when it could have been subtly arranged to herald a transition into the emerging structure...

A review of the needs of decision makers can also provide insight into the long-term assessment of the organization. Organizational direction is in part shaped by the personalities of those at the helm. If, for instance, top managers possess intense needs to win, corporate direction will likely be marked by assertion in the marketplace.

ASSESSMENT OF THE ORGANIZATIONAL CULTURE

So far, we have examined two perspectives for assessing the organization—identifying gaps and looking at what's to come over the long term. A third perspective is to examine the culture of the organization. Culture includes the norms, values, myths, beliefs, and philosophies that make the organization unique. Part history and part present practices, culture is the context within which the organization meshes people, systems, and resources to achieve a mission in the marketplace.

Few anthropologists have achieved the stature and popularity of Margaret Mead. Not only was she a brilliant scientist, but her work has been useful to our own culture in better understanding itself. It has enhanced communication and broadened understanding. Central to Margaret Mead's way of looking at the world was her unique ability to couple a cold objectivity with a warm compassion. The synergy of these two faculties enabled her not only to "see" a culture, but to feel it as well. She possessed the ability to combine a "separate from" position with a "kindred with" position, a detached objectivity with a human empathy. Her way of looking at the world coupled realness with reality.

You have the capacity to assess your organization like a competent cultural anthropologist. Four perspectives will be presented for your use. The first is assessment through analogies. You begin by symbolically going up 50,000 feet, to view your organization with a kind of detached objectivity. Consider each perspective carefully, jotting down your thoughts in the space provided.

...through Analogies

The use of sports, seasonal, or literary analogies can help spark new views of your organization, fresh perspectives for understanding the unique culture that is your organization.

If your organization were a sport or game, what would it be? Chess, rugby, roulette, bridge, tennis, hang gliding? What season of the year? What novel or play best characterizes the drama played out in your organization? *The Old Man and the Sea? The World According to Garp? War and Peace? Stop the World, I Want to Get Off?* What kind of music? A slow waltz, hard rock, progressive jazz? Write your thoughts in response to these questions in the space below.

ANALOGIES EXERCISE

...through Norms

The second technique useful in assessing your organization's culture is to scrutinize its norms. List four norms of behavior—unwritten but accepted "rules"—that exist in your organization. Examples might be how you are expected to address senior managers, dress codes, how you act in a meeting, topics not to be discussed outside one's department. Jot down the evidence (data element) you have for the existence of each norm.

NORMS EXERCISE

Cultural Norm	Evidence (Data Element)

...through Life Stages

Part of a cultural assessment of an organization takes its life stage into account. Figure 4 is a model developed by Gordon Lippitt in his work

Figure 4. Stages of Organizational Development

STAGE	CRITICAL CONCERN	KEY ISSUE	CONSEQUENCES IF CONCERN IS NOT MET
B I R T H	1. To create a new organization 2. To survive as a viable system	What to risk What to sacrifice	• Frustration and inaction • Death of organization
Y O U T H	3. To gain stability 4. To gain reputation and develop pride	How to organize How to review and evaluate	• Reactive, crisis-dominated organization • Opportunistic rather than self-directing attitudes and policies • Difficulty in attracting good personnel and clients • Inappropriate, overly aggressive, and distorted image-building
M A T U R I T Y	5. To achieve uniqueness and adaptability 6. To contribute to society	Whether and how to change Whether and how to share	• Unnecessarily defensive or competitive attitudes; diffusion of energy • Loss of most creative people • Possible lack of public respect and appreciation • Bankruptcy or profit loss

on organizational effectiveness.[9] It aids in understanding the different concerns and key issues organizations face as they progress through three developmental stages—birth, youth, and maturity.

[9]See, for example, Gordon L. Lippitt, *Organizational Renewal* (New York: Appleton-Century-Crofts, 1969).

Write your answers to the Life Stages Exercise in the space provided.

LIFE STAGES EXERCISE

Using Lippitt's model, what life stage fits your organization?

What evidence or data elements do you have to lead you to this conclusion?

What are the key issues decision makers in your organization will have to resolve as you move to the next life stage?

How can your goal be positioned as a tool or resource to help move the organization to the next life stage?

...through Growth Phases

The fourth and final technique to aid you in your assessment of your marketplace is based on a model developed by Larry Greiner at Harvard.[10]

---

[10]Larry E. Greiner, "Evolution and Revolution as Organizations Grow," *Harvard Business Review*, July/August 1972, pp. 37-46.

Greiner holds that growing organizations move through five very distinguishable phases of development, each containing relatively calm periods of growth which end with some type of management crisis (figure 5). Since each phase is so strongly influenced by the previous one, your sense of your organization's place in its history can anticipate the next development crisis so that your goal could be positioned as a way to help bridge the gap.

Figure 5. The Five Phases of Growth

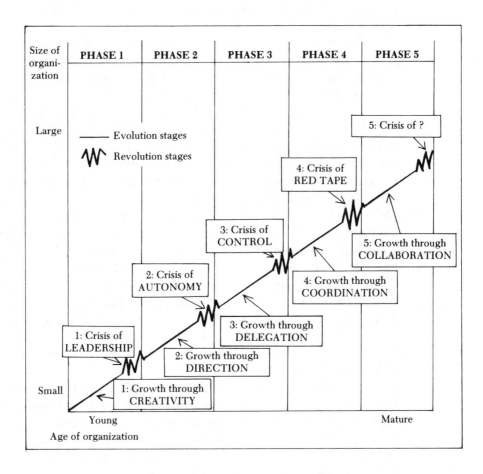

Greiner refers to *evolution stages* as being periods of growth where no major upheaval occurs in organization practices. *Revolution stages* occur when there is a great deal of turmoil in the organization. The amount of time between stages is a function of several factors. The greatest seems to be whether the organization is in a high growth, medium growth, or low growth industry. The higher the rate of growth, the more quickly the stages occur.

Organizations in the first phase of growth, Creativity, are characterized by informal structure and a highly individualistic and entrepreneurial style of leadership, with a "make-and-sell" management focus. Rewards come largely through ownership. The creativity that got the organization started must now be replaced by strong business management.

The second phase, Direction, is characterized by centralized and functional structure, more directive leadership, and development of explicit standards, with rewards occurring largely through salary and merit increases—the focus is on efficiency. Centralized leadership leads to demands by lower level managers for greater autonomy.

The third phase, Delegation, generally gives rise to a more decentralized or geographically dispersed structure, with a delegative leadership style at the top. Cost centers become profit centers, and the reward system shifts toward greater use of individual bonuses. The focus is on expansion, new product development, and acquisitions. Delegation is then carried too far, and top management seeks to regain control from autonomous field managers running their own shows.

Organizations in the fourth phase, Coordination, typically treat line-staff and product-service groups as investment centers. Consolidation becomes the focus, as top management assumes a watchdog style. Rewards gravitate more toward profit sharing and stock options, as the entire planning process becomes more formal and closely monitored. Expanding coordination systems and programs soon overstep their usefulness, resulting in excessive red tape and resentment of staff by the line.

The fifth phase of growth, Collaboration, has the organization's focus shifting to innovation and problem solving. Leadership becomes more participative; task forces and matrix arrangements dominate as the characteristic organizational structures. Rewards gravitate toward the form of team bonuses; mutual goal setting occurs as managers are trained in teamwork and conflict resolution.

Greiner labels the fifth-place crisis stage with a question mark because no organization has yet reached that point. He anticipates the fifth-phase revolution will center around the "psychological saturation" of employees who become emotionally exhausted by the intensity of teamwork and pressure for innovation.

GROWTH PHASE EXERCISE

Given the descriptions adapted from Greiner's article, at what growth phase is your organization?

What things are happening in your organization that lead you to that conclusion?

How can your goal help the organization move quickly through its present or upcoming revolution?

How can your goal aid decision makers in your organization in coping with the next revolution phase?

There are many perspectives helpful in conducting a comprehensive assessment of the needs of the organization. I hope the perspectives presented here have enriched your understanding and sharpened your focus on your marketplace.

Several vantage points have been laid on the table for your perusal and use. We started with identifying gaps between form and substance, examined long-term needs, and concluded with a cultural assessment using four techniques—analogies, norms, life stages, and growth phases. All organizations contain the three dimensions we have explored—current reality, a future perspective, and a cultural milieu of norms, values, and beliefs.

It is now time to consolidate all you have learned in Step 5. Review what you have written. Let it settle in your mind. Now, write your interpretations of the organization's needs or desires on 3" x 5" note cards to be used later.

Just as assessing decision maker needs gave you a leg up on understanding your consumer, assessing the organization aids in appreciating your marketplace. The next step in the process— assessing you—will round out the comprehensive assessment needed for constructing a relevant strategic plan for influencing.

5

ASSESSING YOU, THE SELLER

"You!" said the caterpillar. "Who are you?"

—*Lewis Carroll*
Alice in Wonderland

When you assessed your decision makers, reviewing the principles of human behavior in chapter 3, no doubt you applied some of what you learned to you. This chapter will focus exclusively on assessing your needs—a kind of personal review.

We are all occasionally guilty of letting our needs get in the way of our effectiveness. Our intense need to win, for example, might cause us to try to run the mile like the hundred-meter dash—and we collapse halfway around the track. Our need to be liked may cause us to delay following up with an associate because the follow-up may involve criticism or conflict—and we are unwilling to risk introducing it into the relationship. The need to be perfect may cause us to blow deadlines while doggedly pursuing "perfection." The point is, our own needs can cause us to construct an influence strategy that needlessly risks a negative decision—unless we recognize that possibility and take steps to counteract it.

The next step in the assessment phase is to assess your own needs (Step 6). *You* are the last source of data you will tap before identifying the problems and opportunities upon which you will devise your strategy for presenting your goal to the decision makers.

There are many ways to raise up the cover on our selves to peer beneath. Bookstore shelves are lined with self-help books telling us about our erroneous zones, scripts, OK-ness, games we play, how to be our own best friend. Self-assessment is a critical step for the adroit, effective influencer. Unlike Mary Smith, who had no idea she lacked the interest or ability to supervise, you can avoid getting into situations that hold little or no promise—if you do an initial examination of your own needs, preferences, desires.

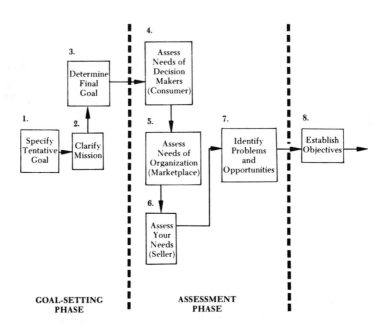

An important principle in marketing, and life, is to recognize that you cannot be all things to all people. The heyday of the Renaissance person and the general store is gone, giving way to narrowly defined experts and specialty shops. An outgrowth of this fact is the requirement to *target market*—narrowly defining the market in order to tailor appeal. If we "general store" our approach to influencing, we risk not only missing the mark in responding to specific needs, but, like Mary and Bob Smith, we also court failure by getting into water swifter than we can handle.

This chapter is aimed at helping you more narrowly define your market through better understanding your assets and liabilities. The objective is the effective matching of self with opportunities. A part of your winning at influencing key decision makers involves finding balance within yourself and between you and your endeavors. Finding balance for yourself is like playing a pinball machine. If you simply watch the machine while the ball makes its round, your score will be low. On the other hand, if you shove the machine too hard, the tilt light goes on and the game's over. Influencers who go for broke often go broke.

The model in figure 6 encompasses four dimensions of self-assessment—may, can, need, and want. Each dimension implies different major issues for you to explore.

The "I may" part of self raises issues of *permission*; the "I need," issues of *responsibility*; the "I want," issues of *interest*; and the "I can," issues of *ability*. The model is simply a tool, a straightforward four-

Figure 6. The Self-Assessment Model

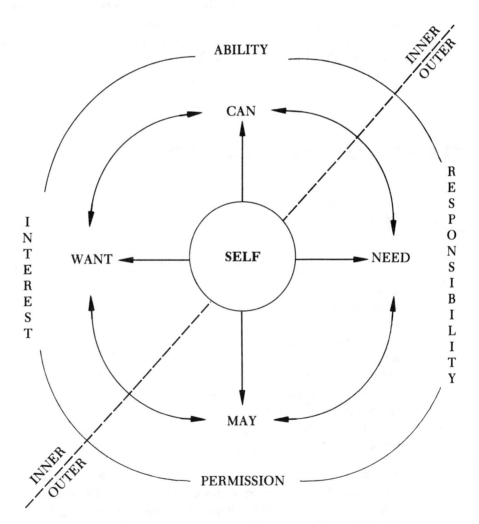

sided picture of self designed to minimize gaps in self-assessment, to help avoid overlooking some major point.

The arrows in the model indicate how the four dimensions (may, need, want, and can) are interrelated. For example, what I am *permitted* to do is clearly related to what I am *able* to do. What I *can* do affects what I *want* to do. Interests are, in part, born out of ability. All of us are prone to say, "I'm really not interested in doing that," when, if the truth were known, the fundamental reason may have less to do with our interest and more with the subtle perception that we lack the ability to do it. We gravitate toward those things which we can do well. The model also illustrates the inherent tensions among the four dimensions. "Want" is in tension with "need"; "may" is in tension with "can."

We will now explore each part in depth as a framework for assessing self. Before beginning, you may want to have your package of 3″ x 5″ cards nearby to record your answers to the questions in the exercises that follow. This will afford an easy, quick review at the end of this chapter.

"I CAN"—ASSESSING ABILITY

"I Can" is the first exercise for your self-assessment. My recommendation is that you find a quiet place to contemplate your answers. You might try writing each answer on a 3″ x 5″ index card, or you can list your answers on a sheet of paper. I will be asking you to come back to them later in this chapter.

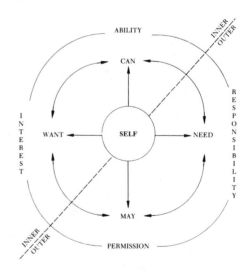

Read each question in the exercise. As you read a question, let your mind wander for a few minutes and then briefly record your thoughts. The key to getting the most out of all the exercises in this chapter is to get out of the way of your mind to let it do the exploring. (Ah! Sometimes easier said than done...)

"I CAN" EXERCISE

1. What is the most important thing you have accomplished in your work life?

2. What are three things you would like to be remembered for were you to die today?

3. What would your close friends acknowledge you were very good at doing?

4. When you felt really good about your work, what was occurring?

5. The thing that angers you most is when people...

Having done the "I Can" Exercise, move to the one on the next page. First, read the list of traits. Then select about six words from the set of thirty-eight which you feel close associates would likely use to describe you.

SELECTING PERSONAL TRAITS

builder	_____	active	_____
opinionated	_____	controlled	_____
imaginative	_____	warm	_____
fair-minded	_____	sensible	_____
popular	_____	fascinating	_____
casual	_____	determined	_____
reserved	_____	compassionate	_____
orderly	_____	executive-like	_____
thinking	_____	matter of fact	_____
peacemaker	_____	correct	_____
critical	_____	talkative	_____
quiet	_____	punctual	_____
lively	_____	easygoing	_____
firm	_____	careful	_____
appealing	_____	detached	_____
systematic	_____	scholarly	_____
judgmental	_____	arrogant	_____
intellectual	_____	considerate	_____
tidy	_____	angry	_____

Your answers to the questions in the exercise and your word choices from the trait list provide a collage of intimate information, as yet unfinished. Your responses are the raw material, the data elements, for your self-analysis—like Tinkertoys™ scattered on the floor just waiting to be assembled into a usable product.

My recommendation is that as you scan your notes or cards you look for patterns, similarities, or themes. As you do, you will be aware that the images are telling you about your abilities as well as about those psychological needs and drives that are distinctively you.

Abilities and Liabilities

Before going further, be aware that for any ability there is a corresponding liability.

Let's presume that in looking over your response cards, you noted that your strengths included the ability to make people feel comfortable. You checked adjectives on the word-choice list like *popular, casual, forgiving, easygoing,* and *appealing.* Perhaps you are known as a peacemaker, someone who is caring, friendly, and considerate. The advantages of these characteristics are that they enable you to feel comfortable and confident when dealing with people. You probably have satisfying relationships, and a wide circle of friends. However, the flip side of this strength is the fear that you will be disliked, unaccepted, and disapproved of.

Another example would be to suppose your assets included a strong need to achieve, a strong desire to win, to be the best, to always get the job done better than anyone else. You checked words like *active, determined, executive-like, builder.* Those assets carry with them the fear of not measuring up, the fear of failure.

I point this out because a part of self-assessment includes gaining awareness of both your abilities and your liabilities.[11] Knowing that my strength in dealing with people carries with it a fear of rejection enables me to better predict how I will react when conflict occurs. With this awareness, I will less likely be debilitated by that conflict; I will be better able to acknowledge my discomfort and manage my fear.

So what if I have a fear of rejection, or a fear of failure, or a fear of losing control or being dominated? What has that got to do with influencing? I think it has a great deal to do with it. Before proceeding with an influencing strategy, I have to decide what market I *can* obtain. The issue here is not permission, but ability. For example, if I am aware that the world is experiencing a shortage of piano tuners, I recognize the need for piano tuners, and I know that I have permission to be a piano tuner, but if I am tone-deaf, my energies might be better directed toward another market!

---

[11]There are numerous personal assessment tools on the market that can be used to get an even better reading—I highly recommend you try some of them. Some of the instruments that have been useful to me include the *Myers-Briggs Type Indicator* (Palo Alto, Calif.: Consulting Psychologists Press, 1962), the *Edwards Personal Preference Schedule* (New York: The Psychological Corporation, 1952), and the *FIRO-B* (Palo Alto, Calif.: Consulting Psychologists Press, 1977). Most counseling centers are equipped to administer such tests and provide a useful interpretation of the results.

> *ONLY CONNECT.*
>
> *—E.M. Forster*
> Howard's End

After you put together a self-profile, one thing that is useful in self-assessment is to get some confirmation on the accuracy of your impressions by disclosing yourself to others. Seek out people you feel confident will be honest with you and ask for their reactions.

Another way to confirm your impressions is to recall a series of past incidents and try to remember how you acted. How we functioned in the past is often our best clue to how we are likely to behave in the future. Go up 50,000 feet and examine *you.* Verify your self-profile hunches with real data from the past.

Think, for example, of the last party you attended. How did you act? Think about the last meeting in which you were in charge. How did you act? Think about the last time you were with power figures. What did your body tell you was going on? How do you have fun when you get to choose what you want? What do you read? Do you read books which are realistic or romantic?

Take five minutes and reflect on what you wrote in the "I Can" exercise and the thoughts you have had about your abilities and liabilities. After doing so, complete the Abilities/Liabilities Exercise. It will be a record for you to use later in this chapter.

ABILITIES/LIABILITIES EXERCISE

I believe my greatest abilities are:

I believe some of my liabilities include:

Now, go back and review your list of abilities and liabilities in light of your influencing goal. Circle the strengths most useful in influencing those making decisions on your goal. Circle the liabilities that pose the greatest threat to your influencing plan. In the space below, list four ways you can use the abilities circled to eliminate or compensate for the liabilities you circled. After writing them here, make summary statements on your 3″ x 5″ cards.

ABILITIES USEFUL IN INFLUENCING

1.

2.

3.

4.

We will now explore the next part of the self-assessment model— "I May." However, we will return to the question of abilities later.

"I MAY"—ASSESSING PERMISSION

There is a dynamic tension between "may" and "can." Although closely related, they make strange bedfellows. The reason is that our sense of what we are *permitted* to do is often clouded by what we are *able* to do.

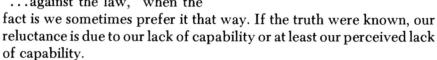

Permission sometimes provides a convenient cop-out for not doing what we in actuality are unable to do. We say, "I wish I could but I'm not allowed to," or "It's against the rules," "...against the norm," "...against the law," when the fact is we sometimes prefer it that way. If the truth were known, our reluctance is due to our lack of capability or at least our perceived lack of capability.

I once knew a nine-year-old boy who told his friends he wasn't allowed to go out for football because his mother was afraid he would be hurt. The football coach suspected there might be different reasons, because he knew the boy's father had been a championship football player in college. In talking in depth with the boy, he learned the boy really wanted to play football but he was afraid he would not be able to measure up to his father's high expectations of him as an athlete. "I can't" often turns into "I am not permitted to."

"I MAY" EXERCISE

Think of two work situations for which you can clearly say you were not acting in the manner you would have liked because you did not have permission. Describe each of them in the space below.

1.

2.

Now, answer the following questions in relation to the two situations above. You may choose to place your answers on 3″ x 5″ index cards.

1. Who prevented me from doing what I felt I needed to do in each situation?

2. What reasons does that person have for being an obstacle?

3. Can I look at each situation from a different perspective so permission is not an issue?

4. What would have happened if I had ignored the question of permission and done it anyway?

5. Am I confident that I would know what to do if permission were not the issue in this situation?

6. Were there barriers other than permission?

⇩

7. Consider a few other situations. Are there many in which permission is a barrier to my doing what I feel should be done?

If so, what can I do to alter the pattern?

> *Once upon a time, Federal Reserve Board regulations required that a secured loan be backed by listed securities equal to five times the value of the loan. When Kirk Kerkorian approached a large bank to finance his acquisition of MGM studios, he encountered a problem. Obviously, the enormous cost of a major company like MGM meant few people in the world would have securities equal to five times the value of the loan. The bank refused to grant permission.*
>
> > *Kerkorian was undaunted. He called upon two of his abilities and compensated for one of his liabilities; he kept his quick temper in check, while trading on his super financial acumen and his ability to get his adversaries to help him solve his problem. He got the bank to agree to alter the concept of the financing he required. They completely circumvented the historical permission issue around a secured loan. The bank advanced him the five million he requested based on a new concept called an "unsecured loan"!*

What does permission have to do with effective influencing? My experience has been that staff professionals need to be clear on any hang-ups they may have regarding authority. It is best to be free of self-imposed internal restrictions. Eleanor Roosevelt once said, "No one makes you inferior without your permission." My friend Stan Herman says, "No one gives you freedom; you are free if you are free." Freedom is essentially the state of mind that says you are free and internally unencumbered. There may be restrictions, but they are external, not internal.

When the highest ranking authority in your organization enters your office, do you feel fear or anger? Anxiety? Joy? Does your face flush or a hot feeling come to the pit of your stomach? How open are you in leveling with your parents? How straight are you in responding to your boss about your true opinions?

One thing you may see at this point is that, just as ability has two sides (ability and liability), there are two ways to look at a question of permission. One is to see whether permission is the real question, the other is to determine whether something else disguised as permission may be at work.

When permission is clearly involved, the next thing to consider is how you deal with it. This relates to how you respond to the dynamics of power, authority, control, and dominance. Only out of an awareness of your likely responses can you manage the situation rather than being controlled by it.

In summary, take five minutes, lay this book aside, and think about how you have responded throughout your work life to the "May I's," the permission questions you have had to confront. People are autonomy-seeking creatures. Recognize that part of being human is to resist being controlled. Some of us resist more than others. As the old Jesuit saying goes, "It is easier to ask for forgiveness than to ask for permission."

The manner in which you cope with permission issues is an important key to your effectiveness in influencing others, particularly decision makers above you. Have you cowered down and blamed? Have you struck back in fury? Have you relented with resentment? Have you asserted your position, then supported a compromise resolution of differences? Consider how you have managed permission situations in the past.

Now, write a few brief notes to yourself about how you can best deal with the permission issues that may be associated with your influencing goal. After jotting down random notes below, summarize your thoughts on 3″ x 5″ cards for later use.

WAYS TO DEAL WITH PERMISSION ISSUES

We will now leave "I May" for the moment and shift our energy to the third part of the self-assessment model—"I Want."

"I WANT"—ASSESSING INTEREST

"I Want" has to do with desire, interest, or preference. As I stated earlier, each part of the model is tied to the others. For example, "I Want" is often dictated by "I May." Interest sometimes follows permission. And, when we are told, for example, "You may not do that," we sometimes retreat by retorting, "I really didn't want to in the first place."

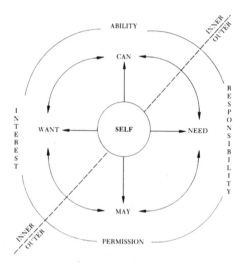

Acting on our interests often involves weighing the satisfaction and dissatisfaction associated with them. As humans, we have a strong motivation for growth. But we likewise have a survival need to avoid pain. Growth often carries pain. Consequently, we are forever in an internal conflict regarding interests.

At one level, our interests promise perpetual satisfaction. Were they not providing satisfaction, they would not be labeled interests. Our interests, likewise, carry the potential for dissatisfaction. There is always a higher level of accomplishment to attain, which pours out of our extensive growth need. As soon as we are settled on an interest, we become dissatisfied if the growth slows. We want to learn more. We want to move forward into a new interest frontier. If I learn to play the piano well (and it is a source of joy), I am exhibiting an interest—but there is always more to learn. Given the strong motivational quality of growth itself, it may be useful to examine interests and their associated potential for dissatisfaction when planning an activity that involves growth beyond the current level of accomplishment.

> BRUTUS: 'Tis a common proof,
> That lowliness is young ambition's ladder
> Whereto the climber-upward turns
> his face.
> But when he once attains the upmost
> round,
> He then unto the ladder turns his back,

Looks in the clouds, scorning the
base degrees
By which he did ascend.

—*William Shakespeare*
Julius Caesar
Act II, scene 1

What do our interests tell us about ourselves? Looking at "I Want's" is to isolate those activities, events, and things to which we direct our energy with absolute free will, out of unrestricted choice. You will remember I described how, psychologically, we always have a choice. We never, at the moment of decision, decide on something we think is stupid or ridiculous. Those choices can be revealing.

The questions in the next exercise can be useful in exploring interest. Likewise, it will be useful to explore potential interests not chosen and examine why. Assessment of interest is essentially answering the question: what do I do when I do what I want and why do I do what I want? Review the questions in the "I Want" exercise. You may want to place your responses on 3″ x 5″ cards.

"I WANT" EXERCISE

1. The last time I did something that really made me feel good, I...

2. If I had an unlimited expense account and free time for one month, I would spend the last two weeks of that time...

3. If I could do what I really wanted in my organization I would...

4. What types of activities do I engage in at work when I am not working on a task or work objective?

5. Examine the choices involved in the following:
   - Associations or clubs to which I belong

   - Books I read when I read for pleasure

   - Movies I prefer

   - Types of friends I enjoy

   - Automobiles I like

   - Foods I enjoy

The rationale for the "I Want" exercise is that the patterns of our choices give us a better handle on our personal picture. The reason, for example, that I ask you to look at the movies, books, or cars that you like is that I believe that most of the time we buy or choose things in order to demonstrate we are particular kinds of people (or not particular kinds of people). For instance, if you had unlimited resources for purchase and maintenance, and resale value were not an issue, what kind of automobile would you buy? What statement does your choice make about your interests? Your interests are by and large a peephole into your personality.

In summary, consider your interests. How do they relate to your influencing goal? How can you shape your goal to be even more in sync with your interests? In what ways can you use your interests to influence your key decision makers?

"I Want" is a step toward aligning how you actually spend your energy with how you would prefer to spend it. "I Need" is the final part of the self-assessment picture.

"I NEED"—ASSESSING RESPONSIBILITY

Just as there is a dynamic tension between "may" and "can," there is likewise a tension between "need" and "want." "Need" implies a sense of responsibility, a requirement, an urging. We get a sense of that when someone says, "I really feel called to do this," or "I feel like I really need to do that." The word implies a certain drive and sense of commitment, perhaps even a compulsion.

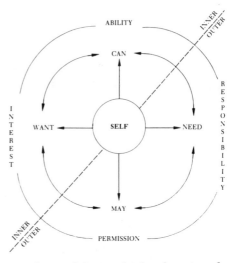

"I Need" has to do with the areas of your life in which other people expect something of you, activities for which you are held accountable. Tension between "need" and "want" comes when we begin to sort out our preferences from our responsibilities. All of us from time to time have made statements like, "I know I *need* to do this, but I'm not really interested." The flip side is, "I really *want* to do something in that area, but I'm not sure it is needed." We are frequently balancing *desire* (want) against *responsibility* (need), trying to find the point where some quantity of each exists. A measure of each is a prelude to action.

Responsibility also has to do with compulsion. Stated in a different way, if you feel guilty about not doing something, you are probably dealing with a need. We sometimes feel we need to spend more time with our children and, sometimes, we *want* to spend more time with our children. It is a sense of obligation that is the basis of need. I need to be more assertive in my dealing with my parents. I need to work fewer hours. I need to contribute more time to my community or more money to my church. I feel so obligated. Since guilt never produces long-term positives, it's important to assess where want stops and need starts.

What you feel you *need* to do can be important introspection in preparing to market your goal within the organization. Review the questions in the next exercise as you have done in previous sections. You may want to put your responses on 3" x 5" index cards.

"I NEED" EXERCISE

1. Below are two circles. Divide circle A into three sections—work, play, learning—based on how much time you devote to each. Divide circle B to show the mix you would prefer.

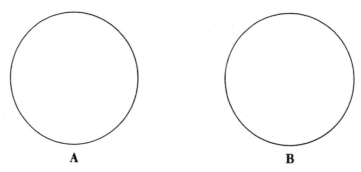

2. List three things you might do which would help change A to look like B (if A and B are different).

   1.

↓

2.

3.

3. List several things you feel you have to do in your life, but would prefer not to do.

4. What can you do to:
   A. Limit some of the "have to's"

   B. Better cope with the "have to's"

5. What aspects of your goal would you really not like to do but feel you must?

6. What can you do to alter the situation described in #5?

LOOKING AT SELF

As you approach the end of this chapter on self-assessment, you will find yourself holding a batch of 3″ x 5″ index cards or a laundry list of statements, paragraphs, words, diagrams. What does it all mean? What will you do with all this? How can such a hodgepodge of information be turned into a practical guide to marketing your ideas in your organization?

My hunch is that many insights have occurred simply as a result of the mental process of responding to the queries posed to you so far. I don't propose to stop here, however. I suggest that you take your stack of cards and go back through them and sort them into common points or paragraphs by finding words that are similar. The sorting process will unveil a mosaic of needs, likes, abilities, and fears—a personal picture, the collection of similarities and contradictions that is you. Your final cards should reflect your strongest needs or desires.

The key to benefiting from this new understanding (or confirmation of what you already knew) is to use it in guiding, monitoring, and redirecting your actions. For example, knowing that you tend to avoid certain situations is valuable. Using that knowledge to eliminate the avoidance, or to appropriately manage your actions around it, is even more valuable.

Blending your knowledge of others' psychological needs (the organization, the decision makers) with the information derived through the self-assessment model produces dynamic data for implementing your goal. It will help you fine tune and target your marketing efforts. Likewise, it will come in handy as you present your idea, proposal, project, or request to the decision makers.

You are an instrument of change. The more you know about that instrument, the better you will be able to use it effectively. The greater familiarity you have with the threads that construct your personal fabric, the more likely it becomes a mantle of strength, security, confidence, and excellence.

6

IDENTIFYING PRIORITY PROBLEMS AND OPPORTUNITIES

*A wise person will make more opportunities
than he finds.*

—*Francis Bacon*

The final step in the assessment phase is the identification of the key problems and opportunities upon which you will fashion your influence strategy; that is, your *course* for greatest effectiveness. In this step, you turn the conclusions you have reached from your assessments into workable form. Following this step, you will move into the marketing solutions phase, beginning with the formulation of strategic objectives.

Let's take a moment to review where we've been. As an example, the sequence of assessment activities you have performed might be pictured as in figure 7. This diagram is different from any you have seen so far; it is simply a tool for helping you get an overview of the procedures and terms to be employed in this part of the process. It also serves as a compressed preview of coming attractions.

You will remember that a *data element* is a single piece of information or evidence which, when coupled with others of a similar nature, results in a *data conclusion*. These conclusions will be combined to form statements of priority problems and opportunities. In the next chapter, priority problems and opportunities will be translated into verifiable objectives which will enable you to draft an influence strategy. Once a strategy is formed, you will be in a position to generate a variety of tactical activities.

So, in our overall framework, you are about to begin Step 7. Step 7 is your chance to compare, cull, and synthesize your data conclusions. At this time, you no doubt have more 3″ x 5″ data cards than you can comfortably manage. By the end of this chapter, they will be in a manageable form. Likewise, you will have weeded out the data and conclusions that will not be useful in constructing your influence strategy.

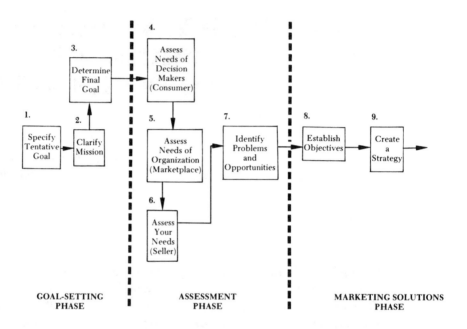

A PERSPECTIVE ON PROBLEMS AND OPPORTUNITIES

An important distinction for proceeding through Step 7 lies in how problems differ from opportunities. Because of the way our minds work, we tend to view a problem as the antithesis of an opportunity. If problems were no more than the opposite of opportunities, or vice versa, then the distinction would be of little use. Thus, a discussion of their true difference is in order. My friend Bruce W. Fritch suggested the following explanation of the distinction.

Figure 7. Assessment Activities Reviewed

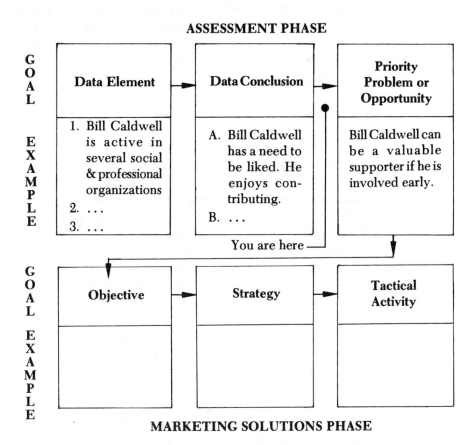

ASSESSMENT PHASE

	Data Element	Data Conclusion	Priority Problem or Opportunity
G O A L E X A M P L E	1. Bill Caldwell is active in several social & professional organizations 2. ... 3. ...	A. Bill Caldwell has a need to be liked. He enjoys contributing. B. ...	Bill Caldwell can be a valuable supporter if he is involved early.

You are here ─

	Objective	Strategy	Tactical Activity
G O A L E X A M P L E			

MARKETING SOLUTIONS PHASE

Your assessment data makes up a sort of "photograph" of the organization, the decision makers, and you. This "photograph" is a static picture at a given point in time. However, it is possible to infer or derive an impression of movement and dynamism from the photograph when you consider it as a point on a trend line—the organization, the decision makers, and you at a particular point in history. Contributing to the sense of movement in observing the photograph is the particular way the mind tends to work with assessment data. As soon as the data is assembled for a forecast, the mind begins to "lean forward," so to speak. Therefore, not only is movement implied by virtue of the photograph's representing a point on a trend line, but when the mind adds past tense (recollection) or future tense (anticipation) to what is being witnessed at a moment in time, the impression of dynamism is strengthened. However, the "photograph," the assessment data, is in fact static.

Given the attitude or viewpoint of the assessor, Bruce suggests, some things assessed at that moment of "snapping the shutter" have a tendency to "rise"—that is, they are considered to be relatively light, vital, healthy. Some have a tendency to "fall"—they are considered to be incomplete, imbalanced, or in poor condition. Those that rise we call "opportunities"; those that fall are "problems." If you "photographed" a high performance automobile, that "data" would rise or fall based on the attitude of the assessor toward such a machine. If speed were king, the car would be an opportunity. When viewed from the vantage point of economy, the car is then clearly a problem. Significantly, whether your mind perceives things photographed as rising or falling when the assessment shutter is snapped depends on the inner motive of the perceiver.

Let's assume, for illustration, that person A desired to increase the size of his or her unit. "What I want is more power!" this person asserts. Person B, on the other hand, takes a wider perspective, seeking to legitimize all of his or her actions within the context of the organization's mission. Person B's actions are contributions; person A's are ploys to gain territory. Person B is "on course"; person A is simply being egotistical. Think how differently these two people would view the exact same assessment data. The difference between their inner motives—"I want more power" versus "What's in the best interest of the company?"—would shape quite different analyses of the same data.

Now, suppose the organizational goal were "by the end of the third quarter, XYZ Company will add forty-eight new stores." The assessment data pertaining to this goal might suggest, "We do not have sufficient staff to meet the training requirements needed to undertake such expansion." The training professional with Person A's motivation will view the condition of the organization or unit to be an opportunity. "Hot dog! I can easily add three new staff members and raise my stature." Person B, being marketing-oriented, will view the same people-short staff and exclaim, "This is a problem which has a high priority and I must address it." Two different orientations yield two different analyses.

It is when you come first from your own agenda—and thus become "not legitimate" in the context of the organization—that viewing a lack of staff resources could be seen as an opportunity. Presumptuousness and manipulation are quelled as we ground our actions in organizational mission.

We have used a power perspective versus a corporate perspective to illustrate the rises or falls which are labeled problems or opportunities. There are many other perspectives which could have been chosen instead of power. Some influencers with high needs for affiliation might view the assessment data in terms of the recognition or acknowledgement they will receive. High-growth-need folks might interpret data as problems or opportunities based on the quantity of learning they will receive. Your self-assessment (chapter 5) will be helpful in determining any personal traps that can "trick" you away from an organizational view.

In the space below, rewrite your priority needs on the left, then translate those needs into any special biases you may bring to data analysis, and jot them down to the right. If you are grounded in corporate mission, you can assign priorities to your actions more realistically.

REVIEWING MY NEEDS AND BIASES

My Needs   **My Special Biases**

DRAWING CONCLUSIONS

We have explored the nature of problems and opportunities and the importance of deriving them from an organization-wide perspective. Priority problem and opportunity statements are formed by the consolidation of your data conclusions. This is aimed at synthesizing your conclusions down to a manageable level.

A way of performing this synthesis is to first array all the cards in front of you and quickly reread each. As you do so, put them into three stacks—one for the decision makers, one for the organization, and one for your own data. Now, take a card from the decision maker stack and compare it to each card in the organization stack. If the comparison yields a problem or opportunity write it on a new card. You will ultimately be comparing every card against every other card.

Let's look at a couple of examples.

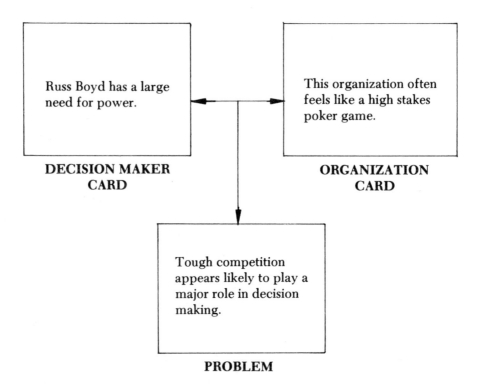

Russ Boyd has a large need for power.	This organization often feels like a high stakes poker game.
DECISION MAKER CARD	**ORGANIZATION CARD**

Tough competition appears likely to play a major role in decision making.

PROBLEM

Given our earlier discussion about the difference between problems and opportunities, you can no doubt envision a perspective in which the problem card might be labeled an opportunity card. Let's take another example:

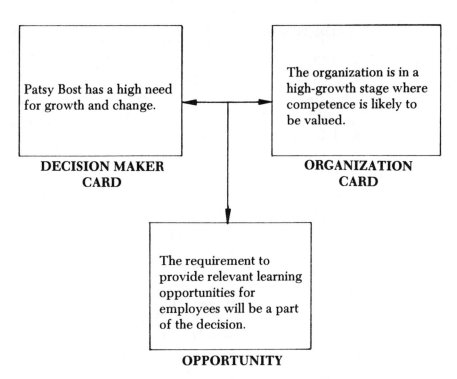

DECISION MAKER CARD

Patsy Bost has a high need for growth and change.

ORGANIZATION CARD

The organization is in a high-growth stage where competence is likely to be valued.

OPPORTUNITY

The requirement to provide relevant learning opportunities for employees will be a part of the decision.

It is now time for you to synthesize your cards. Remember, it is okay to use a decision maker (or organization) card alone as a problem or opportunity statement.

Now, repeat the same process comparing you with a decision maker. For instance:

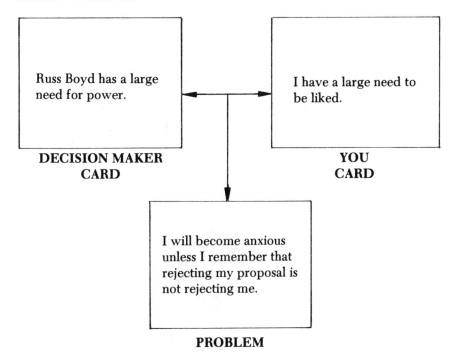

DECISION MAKER CARD

Russ Boyd has a large need for power.

YOU CARD

I have a large need to be liked.

PROBLEM

I will become anxious unless I remember that rejecting my proposal is not rejecting me.

Another example is:

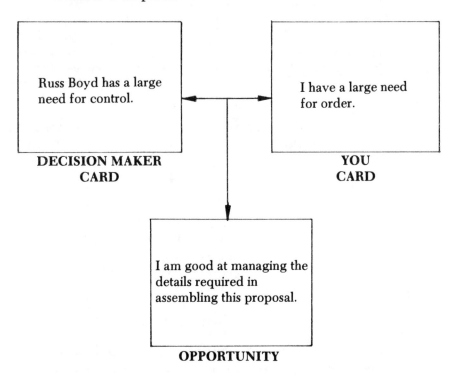

The last comparison is you with the organization. For example:

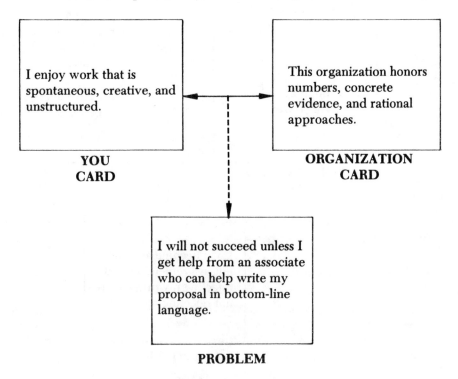

Another example might be:

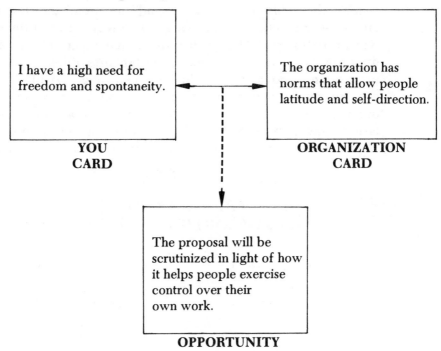

You should now have a stack of problem and opportunity statement cards. You will now make them *priority* statements by culling out those which fail to relate to goal.

USING GOAL TO DETERMINE MARKETING PRIORITIES

Return to your final goal statement which you wrote, aligning it with organization mission (page 31). Read it carefully. With the goal statement firmly in mind (or laid in front of you), review your problem and opportunity statements. Eliminate those which do not relate to your goal statement. You will want to save all those you elect not to use; they may be useful for another goal in the near future. You will be left with *priority* problem and opportunity statements. Write them in the space provided on the next page.

There is an important reason for culling, using goal as the filter. The process will enable you to focus on priority. Since your goal is grounded in organizational role and mission, prioritization helps focus energy, resources, and time fruitfully. Likewise, it assists in appreciating (and therefore adapting to) organizational priorities which exclude your unit.

It could be that you have a big training problem in employees lacking the skills needed to expand the merchandising function. However, given the history of your company, most of the resources will probably go to the mail order department. The problems or opportunities related to mail order facilities might have a higher priority than skills training in merchandising. To plead for skills training resources for merchandising would not be in sync with organizational need since mail order facilities, at this point, have a larger impact on the bottom line. Your goal is to respond, not react. "Pushing the river" is not useful in keeping aligned with the course.

PRIORITY PROBLEM
AND OPPORTUNITY STATEMENTS

USING PRIORITY TO DERIVE OBJECTIVE

You have now completed Step 7 of the influence plan. Your identification of priority problems and opportunities will be invaluable in developing a strategy for influencing decision makers. That laborious process of clarifying goals, aligning with mission, and assessing the key figures in the marketplace will pay off rich dividends in influencing.

You may still be chomping at the bit to devise a strategy and accompanying tactics for influencing decision makers. This process has no doubt tested your patience to the fullest. Have faith that it will produce a sizable return in the end.

There is one last brief step before creating your strategy. This step will be the articulation of objectives. Objectives are the key to completing the process. In the first step in the marketing solutions phase, you will have an opportunity to translate your statements of problems and opportunities into measurable objectives for dynamic influencing.

PART III

THE MARKETING SOLUTIONS PHASE

You have completed the assessment phase of assembling a plan for influencing those decision makers who must "buy" your recommendations. Your assessment activities were aimed at determining who the consumer will be; what the consumer values, needs, and wants; what the marketing setting is like; and your own potential for implementing a plan. You also generated priority problems and opportunities for developing your strategic plan.

The next phase is marketing solutions. As the assessment phase required keen perception and thoughtful introspection, the marketing solutions phase will require creativity and expansive thinking. At the end of the phase, you will have a personalized recipe for functioning as a person of consequence in the game of influencing the decision maker to accept your recommendation.

Marketing and selling are not the same thing. Selling tries to get customers to want what you have. Marketing tries to have what the customer will want—when, where, and in what form. Remember, the marketing approach says that goods and services should be created not merely because something can be sold, but rather out of deep consideration of the needs and wants of possible buyers and potential users. Marketing is no less profitability-oriented than selling; marketing is actually a more managed approach toward ensuring profitability.

Being customer-oriented is different from the old sales-oriented maxim that the customer is king. The word *king* connotes someone in command, who knows what he or she wants and needs, and demands that it be delivered. In many cases, though, customers don't know what they need, certainly not when it comes to the specifics of a product or service. They may want happiness, comfort, mobility, security, and durability, but not know how to get them. They may want specific products and services, but be confused or mistaken about the capacity of these products and services to satisfy their needs. They often have needs they are not aware of and, even when they are, can't necessarily translate them directly into specific wants. They may want one thing, but need another.

Applying the marketing concept to influencing changes in your organization urges you to think in terms of consumer (decision maker) needs in the marketplace of your organization. When there is a need, there is a problem or opportunity. In a manner of speaking, people don't buy products or services; they buy the expectation (or promise) of resolving the need or solving the problem, even the promise of avoiding a problem.

In *Marketing for Business Growth*, Theodore Levitt reminds us: "It is not so much the basic central theme we are selling that counts, but the whole cluster of value satisfactions with which we surround it. It

"I know you're always telling us to sell the sizzle and not the steak, Mr. Bollinger, but just what *is* the sizzle of a 90⁰ elbow flexible copper fitting?"

does little or no good to make a better mouse trap when 'betterness' now has a new, more subtle meaning."[12]

Vance Packard shocked many in the late 1950's with his best-selling book *The Hidden Persuaders*.[13] In it, he not only unveiled some of the more subtle tactics of advertising and packaging, but introduced the mass market to the notion that we satisfy certain psychological needs, motives, and values through the purchase of certain products. For example, he tells the story of how the Ford Motor Company intended to combine the intrigue of the convertible car (a symbolic mistress) with the security of the hardtop (a symbolic wife) in manufacturing the hardtop convertible. True or not, the story illustrates how marketers focus first on the consumer's need or values and then position a product or service as a means for the consumer's satisfying that need or value.

Peter Drucker has observed that organizations have two primary functions: to market and to innovate. Marketing ensures customers are satisfied today; innovation fills the pipeline for tomorrow. *Your* primary functions are very similar. Your ability to market and the relevance of your innovations are forged on the anvil of consumer need satisfaction.

In his *Harvard Business Review* classic, "Marketing Myopia," Levitt describes how the railroad industry failed to view itself from the customer perspective.[14] They thought they were in the railroad business, instead of the transportation business. Their decisions on expansion, routes, railroad cars, prices, people-cargo mix, and so on were made from a product perspective rather than a customer-value-satisfaction or consumer-need perspective.

Hollywood suffered much the same plight. The major studios were practically overrun by television because they considered themselves in the movie business rather than in the entertainment business.

While these examples may sound like they're pointing up trivial semantic differences, the shift in perspective from selling a product or service to one of *marketing an attribute the customer values* is extremely important and powerful. Now, because it is the essence of the point being made, let's repeat that: the shift in perspective from selling a product or service to one of marketing an attribute the customer (decision maker) values is extremely important and powerful.

---

[12]Theodore Levitt, *Marketing for Business Growth* (New York: McGraw-Hill, 1974), p. 47.

[13]Vance Packard, *The Hidden Persuaders* (New York: McKay Co., 1957).

[14]Theodore Levitt, "Marketing Myopia," *Harvard Business Review*, September/October 1975.

7

ESTABLISHING OBJECTIVES

*"Would you tell me, please, which way I
ought to go from here?"*
*"That depends a great deal on where you
want to get to," said the cat.*
"I don't much care where..." said Alice.
*"Then it doesn't matter which way you
go," said the cat.*
*"...so long as I get somewhere," Alice
added as an explanation.*
*"Oh, you're sure to do that," said the cat,
"if you only walk long enough."*

—Lewis Carroll
Alice in Wonderland

Many staff professionals "get somewhere" through continuous rounds of "long walks." The purpose of your influencing plan is to become less involved in long walks and more committed to efficient walks—the "somewhere" being a goal which is valued, important, and rewarding both to you and the organization.

You have identified the priority problems and opportunities derived from a thoughtful assessment of those factors in your marketplace which must be managed for success. The first step in the marketing solutions phase is to translate problems and opportunities into objectives. These will articulate the *what's*, by *when's*, and how *measured*. After establishing objectives, you will, in chapter 8, spell out some of the *how's* (strategy and tactics). We might picture the steps as follows:

- *Why*—mission and goals
- *Who*—assessing decision makers
- *Where*—assessing organization
- *By whom*—assessing you
- *What, when, and how well*—identifying problems, opportunities, and objectives
- *How*—strategy and tactics

Objectives form the link between the *ends* you wish to accomplish and the *means* you have available to use. Setting up the right priorities, knowing when and where to apply effort, gearing effort to results, all depend on choosing the right set of objectives.

Before proceeding, let's review where we are on the influencing model. As before, the preceding step is shown, along with the steps to follow.

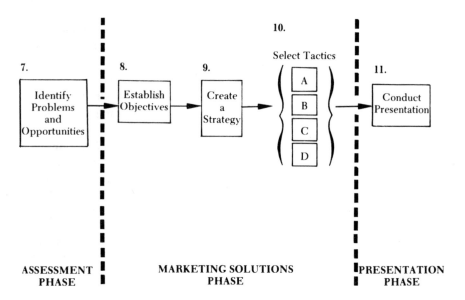

THE ROLE OF OBJECTIVES

Objectives clarify the direction to take in reaching your goal by defining targets or benchmarks along the path to attainment. By establishing objectives, the path to goal attainment is more evident. Implicit in this approach is a plan for overcoming unexpected obstacles or diversions from the path. Armed with clear objectives, you will be better able to determine priorities for action and ascertain methods by which any obstacles or diversions would best be handled.

Suppose you are a mountain climber planning a long hike to the top of a particular mountain (your goal). The path to the top is challenging and demanding. The terrain is not familiar; the obstacles are unpredictable. You want to be at the top on a particular day.

You begin planning your journey by assessing all the maps available, talking with climbers who have climbed this mountain, inspecting your equipment, and checking out your physical condition for undertaking this taxing climb.

You chart a path to the top. Your internal dialogue might sound something like this:

> *"By Wednesday morning, I need to be at this point."*
>
> *"On Thursday by midday, I need to divert from the main path to resupply my water at this stream."*
>
> *"By Thursday night, I must be at this tree line since the morning cloud cover will stop my progress Friday morning, unless I have reached this altitude."*
>
> *"On Friday afternoon, I will be met by a guide who will take me off my path to learn to recognize a poisonous plant which grows on the section of the trail I plan to navigate Saturday."*

We could go on with that example, but I'm confident you see the picture. Objectives enable us to "bend twigs" between here and the destination. Notice that the example contained a collection of problems and opportunities—even a training program en route! Yet, with the goal clearly stated, the destination was always uppermost in the climber's mind.

Climbing mountains and influencing decision makers almost never involve a straight-line path. We can imagine one, but reality rarely matches ideal. There are typically setbacks and sidesteps, deviations and diversions. The purpose of Step 8 in the influencing model is to chart a course which anticipates such contingencies. With measurable benchmarks, we can make our steps more efficient, we can allocate our energy wisely, and we can maintain a clear head about where we are going and where we need to be at any juncture en route. Objectives minimize ambiguity by providing verifiable targets. In essence, they keep the goal and path to that goal in plain view.

An important factor to keep in mind about objectives is that they must be realistic and attainable, but still present a challenge. An objective that is way out of reach causes us to waste energy by struggling against insurmountable odds. An objective should engender stretch without breaking, confidence rather than defeatism. A part of attainability is that they be consistent with the resources likely to be available.

Another important factor to keep in mind is that objectives are not engraved in granite. Objectives represent your best guess as to appropriate benchmarks. You may get down the path only to realize that you need to make adjustments. Stubborn pursuit in the face of facts pointing to flexibility may result in failure to reach the end goal.

WRITING OBJECTIVES

Writing complete, thorough objectives requires attention to three essential ingredients:

1. Spelling out *what* is to be done in verifiable terms. Objectives should be specific enough that you can readily determine whether the action occurred.
2. Spelling out *when* the action will be completed.
3. Spelling out *how to measure* the action.

"You know where I think I went wrong? I never set target dates!"

Reprinted by permission of the Tribune Company Syndicate, Inc.

The priority opportunity in figure 8 was translated into the language of objectives by making it (1) verifiable ("review"), (2) with a target date ("by June 1"), and (3) with some measure ("in sufficient detail to ensure his understanding"). There may be other objectives related to Bill Caldwell with different outcomes and different target dates. Notice the "how" part has not been included. "How's"—solutions—are reserved for strategy and tactics.

Figure 8. Translating Problems/Opportunities into Objectives

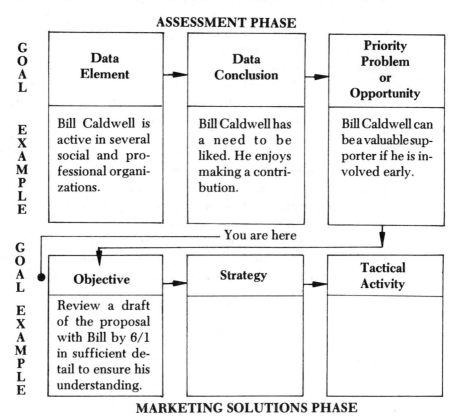

ASSESSMENT PHASE

G O A L E X A M P L E	Data Element	Data Conclusion	Priority Problem or Opportunity
	Bill Caldwell is active in several social and professional organizations.	Bill Caldwell has a need to be liked. He enjoys making a contribution.	Bill Caldwell can be a valuable supporter if he is involved early.

— You are here

G O A L E X A M P L E	Objective	Strategy	Tactical Activity
	Review a draft of the proposal with Bill by 6/1 in sufficient detail to ensure his understanding.		

MARKETING SOLUTIONS PHASE

It is now time to write objectives. Using the format below can assist you in including the key ingredients in a good objective. Take each priority problem and opportunity you have identified and write it as an objective. I suggest you place each objective on a 3″ x 5″ card. This will help in organizing them later. Remember, it may require more than one objective to cover a given problem or opportunity.

WRITING OBJECTIVES CLEARLY		
What	When	How Measured

Once you have spelled out all your objectives, you must organize them. Organization aids in filling gaps and in directing efforts. First, group all cards related to a particular person, unit, activity, or subject. Look for missing steps and add new objectives if needed. Look for redundant steps and eliminate objectives if necessary.

Having culled and critiqued, arrange the objectives in chronological order. Again, note overlap, redundancy, and gaps and correct them. You will be able to create a work plan from this arrangement. As you arrange the cards in sequential order, continue to ask, "Is this objective realistic?" "Can I accomplish what I have written, in the time frame allotted, with the measurability specified?"

This is the last step before developing a strategy. Let us review what you have done.

The priority problems and opportunities you identified are only useful when translated into verifiable objectives. These objectives are the benchmarks along the route to achieving your final goal.

If you took a trip across country, you would not likely point your automobile westward and drive into the sunset. Like Alice in Wonderland, you might end up somewhere, but likely not in the most efficient manner. You, instead, would plan checkpoints to keep you aligned with your destination. You likewise would plan for rest, refueling, and diversion useful in making the trip enjoyable.

The objective of objectives is to structure your plan for influencing in a manner that increases the probability of success. With objectives (the "what's"), you are ready to examine the "how's."

8

CREATING A STRATEGY

One does not gain much by mere cleverness.

—*Vauvenargues*

The word *strategy* is used in many ways by writers and managers. Some use the term to cover "what" the organization will be as well as "how" it will get there. Managers talk about their "pricing strategy," or their "advertising strategy," or even their "planning strategy."

The term *strategy* will be used in this chapter in a very precise way. It is a definition of how you will be *viewed* if you are effective. Strategy defines your distinctive competency to achieve your objectives. It articulates how you will build on the strength of your opportunities to overcome your problems. A strategy is a statement of one's image, an articulation of the position one has selected in the marketplace. It is the filter through which objectives are converted into tactics. As such, strategy takes on a quality-control function.

The marketing concept calls for the influencer to respond to what the consumer wants and needs, rather than trying to persuade the consumer that he or she wants and needs what you have. Great attention is devoted first to determining what the consumer is like, what the consumer desires, and what is your capacity to respond. By inspecting the marketplace, the buyer, and the capacity of the seller, certain problems and opportunities emerge. Problems are barriers to overcome if you are to respond; opportunities are advantages you already have in your capability to respond. These problems and opportunities are translated into objectives—activities for action—which will move you along your path to responding, or contributing.

A marketing strategy articulates how you want the consumer to perceive you as a link to his or her satisfying a need or desire. In other words, your strategy is a statement of your unique qualification for assisting the consumer in meeting his or her need. Your strategy statement will guide you in selecting tactics, action steps, appropriate to your distinctive competency. In this sense, it is a description of how you want to be regarded by the consumer, the decision maker.

You have established your objectives. The tactics you will select will be specific actions for accomplishing those objectives. Because there are many ways to achieve any objective, your strategy will be the standard you will use to select a given tactic.

STRATEGY CREATION: AN ILLUSTRATION

Let's look at an example. In Charlotte, North Carolina, the Fourth Ward—an old residential section nearest the downtown area—had badly deteriorated. Many of the old homes, once stately and beautiful, had been condemned or become havens for derelicts and hoodlums. The city undertook the goal of upgrading the area to attract suburban residents to return to it.

A market assessment determined that many well-to-do residents fancied the elegance of stately old Victorian homes. They also were attracted to the convenience of living close to their high rise offices in downtown Charlotte. Many shared the concern that a once lovely part of town had become a sore spot in an otherwise beautiful city.

Combining government-assisted low interest loans, an aggressive advertising campaign, and personal appeals to individuals known in the community encouraging them to move into the area, the Fourth Ward project got underway. Renovations of the old homes began. Soon, decorative gas street lights, shrubbery lined brick sidewalks, and tasteful mini-parks characterized the area. Luxury townhouse condominiums began to go up. In three years, the Fourth Ward community became a prestige area in which to live. No Sunday afternoon drive with out-of-town guests was complete without a prideful tour of the Fourth Ward.

The strategy of the developers was that Fourth Ward be a community, in the nostalgic sense of the word, that would mix highly concerned, affluent, and educated people who took great pride in their area. This was the distinctive competency the developers communicated to the marketplace.

The story continues. When it came time to construct brick sidewalks in one area of the Fourth Ward—brick sidewalks with granite curbs were an *objective* posited to overcome a problem—the developers needed a tactic for telling residents to move their cars parked along the street. One tactic could have been to place a photocopied notice in each person's mail box or on the windshields of their parked cars. Another could have been to knock on doors the morning of construction. However, since the strategy was to cater to "highly concerned, affluent, educated people who took great pride in their area," the city engineer sent the letter shown in figure 9 to each resident. Notice the following in his letter:

- *Line 4:* "...in order to accomplish this work prior to the Fourth Ward Historical Tour."
- *Line 6:* "...staff...will make every effort to minimize problems..."
- *Line 10:* List of three people to call for questions.
- *Line 15:* "...Mr. Crago will be at the construction site daily and available for your assistance."
- *Line 16:* A twenty-four-hour emergency number for assistance.

Figure 9. The City Engineer's Tactic

OFFICE OF CITY ENGINEER

SUITE 400
CAMERON - BROWN BUILDING
301 S. McDOWELL STREET

City of Charlotte

Charlotte, North Carolina 28204
October 28, 1981

Dear Resident:

On October 26, 1981, Charlotte City Council approved construction of granite curb and brick sidewalk adjacent to your condominium complex. The contractor will be Moretti Construction, Inc..

Construction will start immediately in order to accomplish this work prior to the Fourth Ward Historical Tour. The contractor's staff along with the City's Engineering Department staff will make every effort to minimize problems and inconveniences during construction of this project. We ask your support in this effort to meet this projected deadline by not parking your vehicles in this area during the day.

Listed are the names of representatives of the Engineering Department you may call if you have any questions concerning the construction of this project:

      Dieter W. Crago, Project Inspector   374-2291
      David E. Allen, P.E., Chief Inspector   374-2291
      Steve Moore, P.E., Construction Engineer   374-2291

After construction begins, Mr. Crago will be at the construction site daily and available for your assistance. If an emergency situation should arise at night or weekends, you may call 374-2930 for assistance.

Your cooperation and understanding during construction of this project will be appreciated.

Very truly yours,

C. D. Readling, P.E.
City Engineer

/lb

Figure courtesy of the City of Charlotte, Office of the City Engineer.

The City Engineer did not take the approach of a stereotypical bureaucrat, placing a curt note on the windshield to say, in effect, "Move your car by 9:00 A.M. tomorrow, buddy, or we'll tow it away!" The tactic selected by the City of Charlotte, reflecting the strategy employed for the Fourth Ward area, was extremely advantageous, appealing to community consciousness and written in language pitched to a well-educated reader.

That lengthy illustration above is intended to dramatize how the use of a strategy forms a link between objective and tactic, between "what" and "how," in order to cause the "how's" to appeal to the consumer. That customer appeal is designed to say, "Hey, consumer, I understand you and I know what you want. I'm also the best equipped around to see that you get it. Others may promise to satisfy your desires, but I am uniquely qualified to deliver precisely what you require."

WRITING A STRATEGY

We began this chapter by exploring the meaning of strategy in more depth than we discussed earlier. A strategy is a statement of how you will be viewed by the consumer, the decision maker, if you are to be effective. Before writing a strategy, let's review where we are in the influence model.

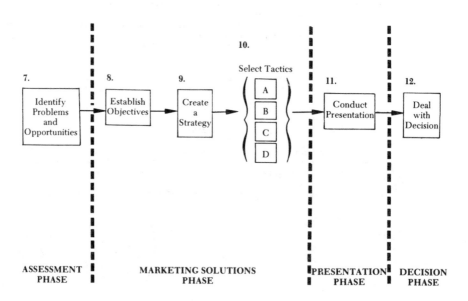

There are a number of ways to create a marketing strategy. One way is to write a statement, in essay form, of precisely *how* you would like the decision maker and the organization to perceive you (or your unit). One unit's strategy statement was as follows:

> *The Training and Development Department will be viewed as a unit which feels continuously responsible for improving the competence of employees to enable them to more productively achieve the organization's mission. The Department will operate in accordance with the premise that all work will be preceded by a thorough needs assessment, conducted with the concurrence of decision makers and managers in those areas to be assessed.*
>
> *When presenting the Department's recommendations, the members of the Department will display a thorough understanding of the client culture. They will likewise display a sensitivity to such concerns as head count, balance sheet, turnover impact, etc. They will ensure that completed work is consistent with the Department's special expertise and with the essential variables of human productivity.*

Another approach is to use feature-benefit statements.

To position XYZ unit as ___[feature]___

so that it is viewed as ___[benefit]___.

A *feature* is a property or attribute of a product, service, or idea. A feature of an automobile could be four-wheel drive, or power windows. A *benefit* is the value the consumer derives from the product, service, or idea. Convenience, beauty, saving time, social esteem are examples of benefits.

Remember that the purpose of writing the strategy is to articulate how you want to be viewed by the consumer so that the consumer sees you as the best resolver of his or her special need. Obviously, you begin by having the intention to be the best resolver. This is why alignment with organizational mission is vital.

The following statements are examples of the feature-benefit approach to writing a strategy.[15]

> *To position the training department as the unit* most concerned *and* most capable of *improving the competence of employees so that the department is viewed as* helping employees function *more* productively *in carrying out the* corporate mission.
>
> **or**
>
> *To position me, the compensation manager, as the person* best qualified *to administer ERISA guidelines so that I am viewed as* keeping the organization from *entering lengthy, expensive* litigation *over compensation disputes as well as from* adverse publicity *in the* marketplace.

Note that each sentence leads with a feature and ends with a benefit. In the process of constructing such a strategy statement, one asserts a distinctive competency which serves as a standard for evaluating tactical actions. The strategy statement is the balance upon which objectives and tactics are compared. Each tactic is thus aligned with an objective and consistent with the strategy.

Remember the Fourth Ward story? The goal was to redevelop the area. One objective was to build a brick sidewalk. The tactic selected for informing tenants to move their autos was consistent with the strategy and helped position the seller, the City of Charlotte, as uniquely expert in satisfying the desires of affluent, well-educated, civic-minded tenants.

---

[15]The reader who wishes additional assistance in using feature-benefit statements to write a strategy might wish to review the techniques described in chapter 9 in "Generating and Selecting Attributes."

In the space below write a draft strategy statement.

STRATEGY DRAFT

Feature   **Benefit**

To position _____ as: So that _____ is viewed
                                        as:

You have the hang of it. Now, write another.

STRATEGY DRAFT

Feature   **Benefit**

In the space below, write a third strategy statement.

STRATEGY DRAFT

If you need a fourth statement, use the space below; otherwise proceed to the next paragraph.

STRATEGY DRAFT

When you have a clearly written strategy, you will have a beacon for guiding you to your destination. When you are in doubt about priority, compare your choices against strategy. If you need to cull activities, cull first those furthest from your strategy. If you need guidance regarding which way to proceed, return to your strategy. It will help keep you grounded in mission and goal.

YOUR INFLUENCING PLAN

Before considering tactics—the activities used to accomplish your objectives, selected after a quality-control check against your strategies—it will be helpful to assemble in one place all the conclusions you have made. Do this by completing Section A of the Final Influence Plan form. Do *not* complete Section B at this time; after completing Section A, skip to the paragraph on page 131.

FINAL INFLUENCE PLAN

Section A

1. My influence goal is (from page 31):

2. The resources I currently have which will be useful to me in accomplishing this plan are (from pages 38, 40, and 41):

3. The priority needs and desires of the decision maker(s) which I need to incorporate into my plan are (from page 149):

4. Key aspects of my marketplace which should be considered are (review chapter 4):

⇩

5. Primary conclusions I must remember about myself as I set out to influence are (page 151):

6. My strategies are (pages 127 and 128):

(to be completed later)

Section B

7. My overall objectives are (review chapter 7):

Tactics I can use to accomplish each objective are:

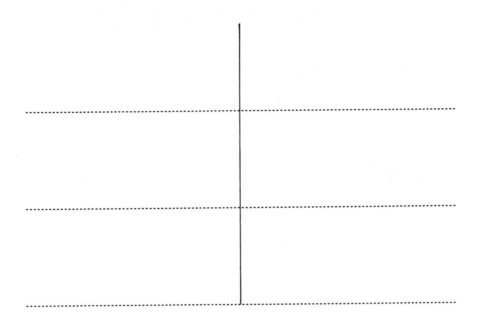

Having created one or more strategies and reviewed the lion's share of your overall influencing plan, you are now ready to devise and select specific tactical activities. Your tactics will eventually be written into Section B of the form here. The tactics you select will be unique to each situation. For this reason, Part IV of this book is titled "A Collection of Tactical Activities." Treat the collection as an arsenal of tools from which to select, depending on what is needed to meet your objectives. Your selections will need to be filtered through your strategies, so read Part IV carefully so you will be completely familiar with the "tools in the box" before completing your influencing plan.

In • flu • ence (in'floo-
ens), *n*., *v*., -enc • ing.

1. the process or

action of producing

effects on others by

indirect or intangible

PART IV

A COLLECTION OF TACTICAL ACTIVITIES

Tactics are specific actions taken by the marketer (influencer) to achieve the objectives. These actions are selected to be consistent with the strategy developed. The objectives are articulated benchmarks along the route to the final goal. These benchmarks relate to opportunities to be employed and problems to be overcome. The priority problems and opportunities are derived from a comprehensive assessment of the marketplace, the buyer, and the capacity of the seller. The goal is carefully attuned to be consistent with and to complement the purpose or role and mission of the organization.

Tactics selected obviously depend on the strategy developed and objectives identified. In Part IV you will find a number of tactical considerations. For instance, an objective used earlier as an example was: "to review a draft of the proposal with Bill Caldwell by June 1st in sufficient detail to ensure his understanding." You will find a tactical consideration entitled "winning advocates" to be particularly appropriate for this type of objective.

The phase in the influencing process immediately following tactics is presentation. There are two chapters on the presentation of a proposal to decision makers—one on how to structure the presentation, another on how to present the proposal. This phase speaks to the selling of an idea or proposal to the buyer.

Our model has been useful in keeping us on the road to planning a success. Let's review where we are.

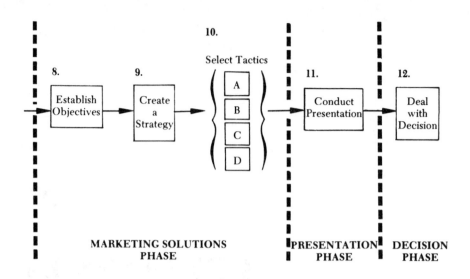

The boxes under Step 10—Select Tactics—are labeled A, B, C, D to symbolically communicate that: (1) generally you will employ a variety of interrelated tactics, (2) what you choose is a function of what you need, and (3) the number of tactics you select depends on what you require. Tactics are combined into your presentation to the decision maker, resulting in an approval/disapproval decision.

As you review the collection to follow, keep two questions in mind:

1. Will this tactic help me achieve one of my objectives?
2. Is this tactic consistent with my strategy?

A GUIDE TO THE TACTICAL ACTIVITIES

Below is a brief annotation of the tactical activities covered in the coming chapters.

Generating and Selecting Attributes

This chapter examines a novel approach for surfacing attributes and then picking those which are most likely to appeal to the marketplace. The techniques presented here can also be useful in developing the feature-benefit aspect of strategy. This chapter comes first because attributes usually govern the other tactical considerations.

Structuring the Proposal Presentation

You will find this chapter particularly helpful in assembling the approach you will choose in presenting your proposal to decision makers. The data you collected during the assessment will be very helpful when coupled with techniques for planning how you will "display" your proposal to the decision maker.

Winning Advocates

Advocates, you will learn, are influence allies. This chapter provides a host of tips on approaches to amplify the appeal of your message by drawing on the advice and assistance of advocates. Your resume of resources, developed earlier, will be helpful to you in identifying potential advocates.

Conducting the Presentation

Drawn from the best thinking on super sales techniques, this chapter reviews how to actually present your message to decision makers. From opening remarks to handling questions, this part covers the basics in the game of selling—an important activity in your marketing approach to influencing.

GENERATING AND SELECTING ATTRIBUTES

*The right answers are not the result of
brilliance or intuition. The right answers
are the result of asking the right questions.*

—Peter Drucker

A useful tactic is to build your proposal around attributes valued by your marketplace and the buyers within it. As we earlier explored in introducing strategy, people do not buy products and services as much as they purchase the expectation that the product or services will satisfy a need.

This chapter is aimed at providing you tools for surfacing attributes (features or characteristics) of your proposal which you can then link to needs identified in your assessment. The chapter is divided into two parts—*generating* attributes and *selecting* attributes. Attribute generation is accomplished by multiplying your perspectives; attribute selection is accomplished by subtracting unworkable attributes by using data gathered in the assessment phase as the standard.

The fundamental task in generating attributes for an influence tactic is to lead from steak to sizzle, from BMW to status, from computer games to winning, from Amway to financial freedom, from Estee Lauder to hope, from backpacks to hearty outdoor fun, etc., etc., etc.

There are many attributes that can be exploded out of your goal. The process I recommend for doing so is aimed at escaping the thought pattern prisons of conventionality. Although, in some ways, it is the most fun part of the process, attribute generation requires the most work. It requires deferred judgment and free association. The purpose is to create a lot of choices early in the game so that you have the freedom later to select ones with a high probability of success.

In its most elementary form, what you are about to do is switch on a green light in your mind and let ideas flow. Then, you will switch on a red light to sort out the ideas which your assessment indicates are most likely to be effective in obtaining a "buy" decision from your consumer.

GENERATING ATTRIBUTES

The purpose of this part, in our planning work, is for you to generate alternate attributes useful in choosing tactics for influencing. The process for accomplishing this will be through effective use of your mind. Before we begin, return to page 31 and read your final goal again. It is very important for you to be quite clear on the result you desire, since it is on your goal that you will focus the creative part of your brain.

Generating attributes is your chance to get a little crazy! Sit back, relax, and let practicality go out the window. We'll get real pragmatic later when we get down to selecting attributes. What I am about to suggest is a largely right-brain, intuitive approach to generating attributes, designed to foster maximum innovation and creativity. Since creativity has often been defined as seeing what everybody else has seen and thinking what nobody else has thought, the tools to follow are aimed at causing your mind to think new thoughts.

Lateral Thinking: An Aid

A fascinating approach to attribute generation is through the work of Edward deBono on lateral thinking. His classic *Lateral Thinking: Creativity Step by Step* is chock-full of useful tips for releasing the mind to produce a creative result.[16] The purpose of thinking is to capture data and use it successfully. Because of the way the mind works to create very fixed patterns of thought, we are limited in our use of new information unless we achieve ways of restructuring the old patterns.

"Vertical thinking" is our logical, sequential approach to problem solving. It is based on proven patterns of thought, and it is useful for

---

[16]Edward deBono, *Lateral Thinking: Creativity Step by Step* (New York: Harper & Row, 1970).

some types of tasks. We will use vertical thinking when it is time to select attributes. "Lateral thinking" is useful in restructuring patterns (gaining insight) and provoking new ones (achieving creativity).

Your mind is a pattern-thinking machine. This means the information-processing system of the human mind acts to create patterns, store them, and recognize those patterns. These patterns are terribly important in communicating. They are like codes. When I say, "Watergate," your mind conjures up a large pattern which enables us to communicate in a shorthand without having to call up every bit of data that made up that mental pattern, "Watergate." We each have our own mental library accessed not by catalog number, but by patterns.

These mental patterns also help us anticipate events. If I top a hill in my car and see a bridge washed out at the bottom, I have a pattern in my mind which, fortunately, makes it unnecessary for me to drive off into the river in order to learn the consequences of "bridge washed out." I complete the action in my mind, so to speak, rather than in my car. In essence, I decide to hit the brakes after extending the pattern.

There are other advantages to having a patterning system. It is a timesaver for the mind. As Aldous Huxley said in his book *Doors of Perception*, "The mind is a reducing valve." Because the mind is constantly overwhelmed with far more information than it can consciously absorb, it must have some system for sorting out specific information. It is the patterns created by previous information (beliefs, values, language, codes, symbols, and so on) that allow the mind to prevent being overwhelmed by a mass of data and thus save time. Words are no more than the beginnings of complete patterns which the mind completes by itself. Think about words like *Globetrotter, rape, bonanza, godfather, Disneyland,* and *Lee Harvey Oswald*. It's not the word that typically enters your mind; a whole complex pattern of events, feelings, values, attitudes, and reactions does instead.

A pattern means a previously "proven" system of thought is preferred over another state. DeBono illustrates pattern preferences in the following way. Study the two figures below.

Illustration on page 27 in *Lateral Thinking: Creativity Step by Step* by Edward deBono. Copyright © 1970 by Edward deBono. Reprinted by permission of Harper & Row, Publishers, Inc.

If you react like most people, your mind responds to the two figures as a partially covered letter *A* and letter *R*. The mind has a lower tolerance for ambiguity and constantly seeks patterns in chaos. In clarifying ambiguity, it may make the wrong assumptions.

Look at the letters below and note how your mind fills in the vacant box.

Your mind no doubt sought to make a pattern. "Ah," you thought, "It could be a *C*. Or is it an *O* or an *I*? If I told you it should be a *6*, you'd probably feel perplexed. We are much more comfortable with known, familiar patterns.

As a patterning system, the mind also has limitations. Foremost is the fact that assumptions are easy. Like AB__DE, we can be seduced into following the dominant path and may, therefore, not easily be aware of other possibilities. Similarly, the best established pattern has complete dominance over any alternative patterns the mind has created. The dilemma, according to deBono, is that a person with a limited repertoire of patterns will be unable to look at data in a meaningful way; a person well equipped with patterns will be unable to look at the data in a new way.

Another limitation stemming from the mind's patterning system is that it is much easier to develop a completely new pattern than it is to cut across an old one, using some part of the old one but exchanging the rest for something new. A patterning system is a probability system. By identifying the first part of the pattern, we bet that the rest will be as expected. If two completely different situations start out the same way, it is very easy to use the wrong pattern 50 percent of the time.

Lateral-thinking techniques can help overcome some of the limitations of the mind as a pattern-making machine. Where there is a pattern, there is a preference; where there is a preference, the freedom of choice needed for innovation is lacking.

Using lateral-thinking techniques forces the mind to work in new ways by providing a means for restructuring, for escaping age-old patterns and for putting information together in a way that *generates* new ideas. The objective is to be provocative rather than analytical, to create instead of choose. The reason I earlier said this was your chance to "get crazy" is that in generating attributes, richness is more important than rightness. We will be evaluating, analyzing, choosing— and be concerned about relevance—in the subsequent step, when you select attributes from the list you generate.

Generating Technique #1: Establish a Quota for the Number of Ways to View Your Goal

This technique is designed to make you stretch, to go past the point you might normally go. Suppose your unit were justifying the purchase of six new flip charts. You might ask your unit to identify *ten* ways the organization could use such equipment. The point is the *ten* helps force your mind into new patterns—you begin leaving the old, established patterns after six or seven.

When one training department actually used this technique on this particular problem, the ninth and tenth ideas were the ones that sold the personnel director on buying the six flip charts. The ideas were: (1) to use flip charts as changeable maps in directing new recruits to their work stations (the company shifted departments around frequently) and (2) occasionally using the flip charts in the cafeteria as a "graffiti wall" for suggestions.

Another training department sought to gain approval for a new customer service training program. Some of the attributes generated using the "establishing a quota" technique were:

1. Increase competence in handling customer complaints
2. Reduce merchandise returns
3. Reduce billing errors
4. Enhance company image
5. Improve interunit communication
6. Surface other customer-related training needs
7. Test the new procedure for handling customer complaints
8. Improve cross-selling skills
9. Distribute new job aids for expediting returns
10. Identify candidates for future supervisory roles

Now, let's apply the technique to your goal.

GOAL ATTRIBUTES

Identify six attributes of your goal. Write each attribute below and on an index card. You may be modifying these and adding others later.

1.

2.

3.

4.

5.

6.

Generating Technique #2: Challenge the Assumptions Associated with Your Goal

Many people have seen the famous nine-dot exercise, which asks you to connect nine dots with four straight lines without lifting your pencil off the paper.

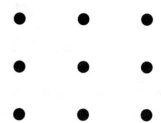

If you have never attempted this exercise, you may want to try it *before reading further*.

People who have never seen the exercise usually have difficulty completing it. The exercise can only be solved by drawing lines that extend outside the box effect created by the nine dots. We assume we must stay within the self-imposed boundaries. (If you have not seen the solution, it is included at the end of this chapter on page 154).

In another example of challenging assumptions, a riddle: A man gets on the elevator each day en route to the fifteenth floor. He rides to the tenth floor, gets off, and walks the rest of the way up the stairs. At night, however, he gets on the elevator and rides to the bottom. *Why?* The answer is he is a dwarf and cannot reach the button for the fifteenth floor. That is, he could only reach up to the tenth floor button. When attempting to solve this riddle, we probably assume, given our pattern of thought with this situation, that the individual was of average height.

The nine-dot exercise and the riddle above illustrate the importance of challenging the validity of our assumptions, the thought constructs that may inhibit our discovery of new alternatives. The objective of challenging assumptions is to break up the old patterns so that new ones can be forged, thus increasing our alternatives for later making the wisest choice. Assumptions are by definition old patterns.

Assumptions are barriers to generation. By examining the ones which exist, we are better able to break through to more attributes. For example, the tactic of getting another staff member typically rests on one or more of the following assumptions:

- The person must be on my payroll.
- The person must report to me.
- The person must be an employee.
- The person must be full time.
- The person must work only on the work from my area.

There are probably other assumptions. If we challenge one of the ones above, we open the door to fresh perspectives—thus new attributes. Challenging assumptions aids us by forging a path to choice.

Think long and hard about your goal. Are there any assumptions you are making about it which could limit its potential for being approved by decision makers? The sources of the dollars needed to fund a new proposed program, for instance, might not be limited to your budget. If the proposed program were packaged, marketed, and sold outside your organization, you might recoup the major expenses.

Use the space on the following page to identify assumptions you may be making about your goal. Then star the ones you want to challenge.

GOAL ASSUMPTIONS

One way to challenge assumptions is to ask a colleague to critique the attributes of your goal by repeatedly asking "why?" It's like a young child who asks a question and then, on hearing the answer, asks, "Why?" As soon as an explanation is given, it is followed by another "why?" Try it with your goal and a colleague. By creating discomfort with any explanation, as the mind continually searches for a new way to explain, the possibility increases that restrictive assumptions are laid bare so that new attributes can emerge. If new attributes do surface, write them on 3″ x 5″ cards.

NEW GOAL ATTRIBUTES

Generating Technique #3: Defer Evaluation of Any Possibility

The use of deferred evaluation, or suspended judgment, is the basis of brainstorming. (Brainstorming is a more formal group procedure for using deferred evaluation.) The notion behind the technique is that it is far easier to tone ideas down than to think them up. In deferring evaluation, we focus all of our energy on generating ideas.

Similar to Generating Technique #1, it calls for your going totally wild for a short time to generate as many attributes as possible—quantity is more important than quality.

The objective of the suspended judgment is not to be right, but to have options. As deBono says, "It is better to have enough ideas for some of them to be wrong than to be always right having no ideas at all.[17] Deferring evaluation, suspending judgment, allows ideas to stay around long enough to set off other ideas. An idea may be obviously crazy but stimulate another which is very practicable.

DeBono uses a story to illustrate. An organization was having a major problem with absenteeism among its assembly line workers. In a brainstorming session designed to generate alternative solutions, someone suggested they keep workers on the job by cutting off their legs. It brought laughter *and* the solution. The company began a program of hiring more handicapped employees. Handicapped people typically have a much lower absentee and turnover rate than others.

Try brainstorming attributes for your goal. Again using 3″ x 5″ cards, write down all the attributes you can think of in fifteen minutes. Put each attribute on a separate card. Remember, rightness doesn't matter, richness does!

Generating Technique #4: Use a Checklist of Trigger Words

Another useful approach in generating attributes is to use a checklist of trigger words to suggest new attributes. A well-known approach is the list on the next page extracted from Alex Osborn's *Applied Imagination*.[18]

---

[17]deBono, *Lateral Thinking*, p. 108.

[18]Alex F. Osborn, *Applied Imagination* (New York: Scribner's, 1963), pp. 229-290.

With your goal in hand, read the phrase in the checklist to see whether it helps you in altering your perspective. The space below the "idea-spurring questions" is for you to capture ideas you may get.

CHECKLIST OF ATTRIBUTE TRIGGER WORDS

Could I...

Put it to other uses? New ways to use as is? Other uses if modified?

Adapt? What else is like this? What other ideas does this suggest? Does the past offer parallel? What could I copy? Whom could I emulate?

Modify? New twist? Change meaning, form, shape? Other changes?

Magnify? What to add? More time? Greater frequency? Stronger? Higher? Longer? Thicker? Extra value? Plus ingredient? Duplicate? Multiply? Exaggerate?

Minify? What to subtract? Smaller? Condensed? Miniature? Lower? Shorter? Lighter? Omit? Streamline? Split up? Understate?

↓

Substitute? Who else instead? What else instead? Other ingredient? Other material? Other process? Other place? Other approach?

Rearrange? Interchange components? Other pattern? Other layout? Other sequence? Transpose cause and effect? Change pace? Change schedule?

Reverse? Transpose positive and negative? How about opposites? Turn it backward? Turn it upside down? Reverse roles? Change shoes? Turn tables? Turn other cheek?

Combine? How about a blend? An alloy, an assortment, an ensemble? Combine units? Combine purposes? Combine appeals? Combine ideas?

If new attributes emerge, write each one on an index card.

Generating Technique #5: Start at the Outcome of the Goal and Work Backward

A company headquartered in a large high-rise office building had a problem with slow elevators. Employees were constantly complaining about rushing to work only to have to stand a long time in the lobby waiting for an elevator.

The company sought advice from four structural engineers. The first engineer suggested they add another elevator. The second suggested they speed up the ones they had. The third engineer suggested they stagger work times so most employees would not be seeking an elevator at the same time.

The last engineer the company consulted had the most creative solution. She recommended they install large mirrors in the lobby. She saw the problem not so much as the speed of the elevators as the impatience of employees; she started with the outcome and worked backward.

Working backward disrupts the original way of looking at your goal to free information that can come together in a novel manner. The objective is to provoke ideas.

Consider your goal. Imagine how things will be after the goal has been approved. What outcomes will your goal produce? Write your outcomes in the space below.

GOAL OUTCOMES

Write attributes stimulated by considering these outcomes on 3" x 5" cards.

Generating attributes can be fun! It also can be work. It requires a blend of inspiration and perspiration. Given our Western allegiance to concrete logic and rational problem solving, it is sometimes difficult to employ the more abstract, illogical, and irrational processes for creative idea generation.

Review your cards of attributes. Edit, cull, and then number them sequentially. Having generated attributes for a tactical plan, the next step will be to make choices. As you have been expansive during the generation phase, you will now become restrictive.

SELECTING ATTRIBUTES

The "think up" stage now shifts to "tone down." Selection is the process of carefully sifting the multitude of attributes to derive solid ones for assembling an influence plan. The best sieve for sifting is the data you assembled during the assessment phase.

We will begin by comparing the needs of the key decision makers with your attributes. While the needs of the organization and your needs are important to your choices, decision maker needs are the most critical for ingenious selection.

In the space provided below, briefly list on the left-hand side the key needs or desires of the decision makers, which you identified in chapter 3. (Refer to your cards from page 58.) Then, select the attributes of your goal which best relate to the key needs. Write the number you assigned to each attribute in the space to the right. Your list should resemble the example shown in figure 10.

DECISION MAKER NEEDS AND ATTRIBUTES

Name	Key Needs or Desires	Attribute Number

Figure 10. Example: Attributes Related to Key Decision Maker Needs

DECISION MAKER NEEDS AND ATTRIBUTES

Name	Key Needs or Desires	Attribute Number
Howard Perdue	Need for control	2, 3, 7
Jack Gamble	Need to look good to others	4, 8, 5
Lisa Williams	Need to contribute	1, 4, 8

Use a similar process for considering the needs of the organization. Review your cards from your assessment of the organization (chapter 4) and list the key needs in the space provided. Select the attributes you think could be potentially important to your marketplace, and list their numbers to the right.

ATTRIBUTES IMPORTANT TO YOUR MARKETPLACE

Key Organizational Needs or Desires   **Attribute Number**

Next, review the 3″ x 5″ cards that outline your needs and desires. List all the attributes important to you in the space on the next page.

ATTRIBUTES IMPORTANT TO YOU

Your Key Needs or Desires   **Attribute Number**

The next space is for recording those attributes you think may not exactly fit a decision maker, organization, or you, but could be important anyway. List the numbers of those attributes here.

ADDITIONAL IMPORTANT ATTRIBUTES

It is now time to consolidate your selections using the Attribute Selection Matrix. In the matrix, there are two blocks in the column for the primary decision maker since that person's needs or desires should be given greater weight than the other factors. There are blocks for three additional decision makers, as well as for the organization, you, and your list of additional attributes.

Beside each attribute number, enter checkmarks to show whether you identified it with a decision maker's needs or whether you associated it with the organization or yourself. If you included a particular attribute in your list of additional important attributes, put a checkmark in the second to the last column. Be sure to put two checkmarks in the first column for any attribute associated with the primary decision maker. Your final version will look something like figure 11.

Figure 11. Example: Using the Attribute Selection Matrix

Attribute Number	Primary Decision Maker	Other Decision Makers A B C			Organi-zation	You	Additional Attributes List	Total
1	✓ ✓	✓			✓	✓		5
2			✓		✓		✓	3
3	✓ ✓	✓	✓	✓		✓		6
4			✓	✓				2

Once you have entered all your checkmarks, count the number each attribute received and enter the total in the far-right column. Remember that each attribute associated with the primary decision maker receives two checkmarks.

In the space provided on page 154, write out the eight to ten attributes receiving the most checkmarks. These will be attributes around which your influencing plan can be constructed.

ATTRIBUTE SELECTION MATRIX

Attribute Number	Primary Decision Maker	Other Decision Makers			Organi- zation	You	Additional Attributes List	Total
		A	B	C				
1								
2								
3								
4								
5								
6								
7								
8								
9								
10								
11								
12								
13								
14								
15								
16								
17								
18								
19								
20								

FINAL LIST OF ATTRIBUTES

1.

2.

3.

4.

5.

6.

7.

8.

9.

10.

The solution to the nine-dot exercise:

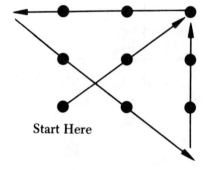

Start Here

10

STRUCTURING THE PROPOSAL PRESENTATION

What a piece of bread looks like depends
on whether or not you are hungry.

—Jallaludin Rumi,
13th century Sufi poet

An important tactical consideration is the structuring of your proposal presentation. You may choose to introduce your consumer to your "product" by means of a written report. The presentation may be a formal event with a group (e.g., an executive committee meeting in the boardroom) or an informal dialogue with a single decision maker. Regardless of the forum of introduction, how you prepare, package, and present your proposal are major considerations.

Many excellent proposals have been disapproved, not because of their substance, but because the presenter failed to employ the form the decision makers preferred. Buyers (decision makers) have been oversold and undersold. Sellers (staff professionals) have mistakenly used graphs and figures before a nonfigures-oriented audience, used technical jargon when plain words would have told the story better, and used dog-and-pony showmanship when it wasn't show time— errors all stemming from the lack of a coherent plan for influencing.

Remember, strategies are the broad plans for influencing; tactics are the specific activities used in accomplishing those plans. A strategy might be "to appeal to Tony Lay's need to help others." A tactic for such a strategy might be to "let him know that 325 jobs will be created by this proposal, reducing the unemployment of Winder, Georgia, by 25 percent."

LOOKING BACK TO PLAN AHEAD

Your first important source of information is your previous experience with proposals submitted to the decision makers. (If you have no such experience, you might want to skip to the next section, "Exploring Alternatives.")

Analyze the successes or failures which you or others have experienced in the past to ascertain why they occurred. What questions did the decision maker ask? What supporting information was requested during the presentation? Did the questions suggest impatience, an awareness of time slipping by? If a group was involved, who *really* made the decision? Could the time of day have made a difference? If a written proposal was submitted, what sections did the decision maker mark up? What additional information or supporting materials might have been helpful before the presentation meeting? What information did they request *after* the proposal was presented?

Reflecting on your previous presentations and the questions suggested above, jot down your thoughts in the blanks below. Identify key lessons from the past which you might need to remember in planning your upcoming presentation.

KEY LESSONS FROM PREVIOUS PRESENTATIONS

EXPLORING ALTERNATIVES

The next step is to consider alternatives for presenting the proposal. The ones listed in the checklist below are the beginning of a list you can build as you use this process repeatedly. Space has been provided for additions. Place a check beside any which have merit for your strategy for your present goal.

PRESENTATION ALTERNATIVES CHECKLIST

_____ 1. Consider presenting your proposal to each decision maker individually before presenting it to them as a group. Decision makers rarely enjoy surprises when it comes to business decisions.

_____ 2. Consider the best time of day to present your proposal.

_____ 3. Consider having someone other than yourself make the presentation.

_____ 4. Consider the right location to make your presentation (off-site instead of on-site, conference room instead of board-room, cafeteria instead of office, etc.)

_____ 5. Consider coupling your proposal with another proposal you know will be a sure winner. The momentum of green light decisions may spill over to yours.

_____ 6. Consider sending the decision maker (or advocates) a draft for critique before submitting the final proposal. People rarely walk away from things in which they have invested.

_____ 7. Consider having a compromise position, a point you can fall back to and not lose everything.

_____ 8. Consider a new approach to funding your proposal (a grant, going over budget, line items, cost sharing with other units, marketing externally, changing the rules, etc.)

_____ 9. Consider whether the decision makers are really ready to buy.

_____ 10. Consider whether risking a disapproval on this program starts a chain of events which multiplies the loss to your unit. Better to lose a battle—win the war!

_____ 11.

_____ 12.

_____ 13.

_____ 14.

_____ 15.

SELECTING SUPPORTING DATA

An important aspect of your marketing strategy may be the specific supporting data you use. What the buyer needs to see and hear can be as important as what the buyer needs to know—a subtle distinction which can turn the tide in the affairs of the seller!

In selecting data to support your proposal, remember the power of the printed word. Allen Funt of "Candid Camera" related the episode in which he and his staff essentially closed the State of Vermont simply by placing a highway sign at the state line— "VERMONT IS CLOSED." Due to the power of the printed word, motorists would read the sign, turn their cars around, and drive off to New Hampshire.

Capitalize on past accomplishments. Are you proposing an activity that has been successfully conducted in the past? For example, year before last, you offered a supervisory development program and your proposal seeks to reinstitute such a program. The reaction of previous participants can be valuable supporting data for your current proposal. Even if your proposal is not precisely the same as a previous program, you can point up its similarities to activities that have been successful in the past.

Have you ever been exasperated by those repetitious user-response advertisements that tell us why Ms. Anita Break from Mudpaddy, Montana, swears by a certain brand? Despite their plain vanilla quality, these ads are reinforcing—buyers gain some measure of confidence in knowing that others found the product satisfactory. The confidence produces new customers and, at the same time, increases brand loyalty among old customers. So, testimonials from the users of past programs (the same as or similar to your proposal) may work well as supporting "data" in your presentation.

In your search for supporting data, look also to other organizations that have attempted what you propose and found it successful. If you can gain access to such information, the presentation of highly irrefutable proof that what you propose worked elsewhere in a similar setting can sometimes mean the difference between a "go" and "no go" decision.

Should you locate such data, it is important that the data be credible and its source valued. As the training manager for North Carolina National Bank, my telling a decision maker that Wachovia Bank and Trust had found what I proposed to be effective gained me no points (Wachovia was our major competitor). However, to state that Chase Manhattan Bank or Citibank had found it successful turned the heads of even the most resistant decision maker.

Supporting data could also include pre- and post-test measurements, observations of specific behaviors, indicators of improved productivity, or reduced turnover, each credibly linked to the proposal. In addition to providing supporting data for the proposal presentation, previous users can be actively recruited to help design your marketing strategy, to personally win new advocates, or to influence decision makers.

Think of supporting data that can be useful to your strategy and list it in the space provided on the next page.

ADAPTING YOUR PROPOSAL TO YOUR AUDIENCE

A vital ingredient in your "cooking up" a powerful presentation lies in its being aligned with the needs of the key decision makers. Figure 12 is a ready reference for adapting the structure of your proposal to your audience.

Figure 12. Audience Adaptors

IF THE KEY DECISION MAKERS ARE:	STRUCTURE YOUR PROPOSAL TO BE:
A. Analytical	A. Highly logical
B. Orderly and precise	B. Neatly structured
C. Conceptual; prefer the "big picture"	C. Built around a framework
D. Long-range-oriented	D. Amplified by trends, projections, and predictions
E. Short-term-oriented	E. Related to impact, bottom line

Figure 12 (continued).

F. Highly social, warm, and affiliative	F. Laced with anecdotes, acknowledgements, and accolades
G. Intellectual, abstract, and intuitive	G. Broad-brushed with references to its being on the cutting edge, the vanguard, etc.
H. Uncomfortable with yes-no decisions	H. Concluded with many options
I. Uncomfortable with options	I. Concluded with request for a yes-no decision
J. Perfectionist	J. Neat and accurate, but containing small flaws
K. Skeptical and suspicious	K. Supported by irrefutable proof, high quality references
L. Controlling and power-oriented	L. Interactive and concluded with recommendations

Go back to chapter 3 and review the needs of the key decision makers you identified. In the block below, identify the two adaptors from the right-hand column of figure 12 which best apply to your audience.

PRIORITY ADAPTORS

1.

2.

Now, take five minutes and decide how the two "audience adaptors" can be applied to your goal. Enter your thoughts in the space below.

APPLICATION OF ADAPTORS

11

WINNING ADVOCATES

One's friends are that part of the human race
with which one can be human.

—*George Santayana*

A training manager I know assembled a proposal for mid-level managers in her company. A needs analysis had clearly indicated that this level of management functioned less effectively than they could have and the main reason was they lacked leadership skills. The proposal would require the approval of the company president.

This training manager was completing her M.B.A. degree at the local university. Realizing that the dean of the College of Business was a golfing buddy of the company president, she asked him to review her training proposal.

The dean was impressed and inquired what the president's reaction had been. "He'll get it next week," she replied. "I would appreciate your letting him know what you think of the proposal when you see him." She is convinced her proposal was approved quickly because of the accolades paid it by the president's friend, the business school dean.

Advocates are important influence allies. The advocate is your "friend in court," a person who can serve your goal in several ways. One way is in the manner the business school dean influenced the president of the company in the example above. The advocate functioning in this manner is one who personally knows the key decision makers and can—with a word, note, or letter—encourage the acceptance of your proposal, project, or request.

Asking an advocate to encourage a decision maker to approve your goal carries some measure of risk. Some decision makers resent being "buttered up" by others, even those whose opinions they value. Others may recognize your marketing handiwork and dislike your effort to "stack the deck." Your knowledge of the decision makers in your organization will aid you in making the right judgment call on using an advocate or not. If you do, the key to success is that the advocate *must* be a person whose input the decision maker values.

Think of a person or persons who could influence the decision makers in your situation. Review your list of people resources on page 38. It could be a close friend or co-worker of the decision makers. If you are to influence a group of decision makers (a training committee or the board of directors), the advocate may even be a member of that group.

In the space below, identify up to three candidates for advocates who could directly influence the key decision makers. Then, circle your top choice and state the rationale for that choice.

ADVOCATE CANDIDATES

1.

2.

3.

Rationale for top choice:

A somewhat less direct way advocates can contribute to your influencing plan is to supply you with valuable information about the decision makers. This can be particularly useful when you are attempting to influence a group you know little about.

Several years ago, when I was the training manager for a financial institution, I wanted to expand the training staff as a part of an effort to transform the department into an internal consulting unit. The proposed addition required approval from a committee of the board of directors. I had an acquaintance who frequently briefed this committee, and his insights and information about the setting, the people, their procedures, and so on, were helpful in fine tuning my strategy *and* increasing my personal confidence.

Are there prospective advocates you know who can provide you information useful to achieving your goal? If so, list their names below along with a brief description of how they can be useful to you.

LIST OF ADVOCATES FOR INFORMATION

Name   **How They Can Be Helpful**

The final type of advocate is a person who can provide you needed resources or unusual favors. An example might be the print shop manager who places your proposal at the front of the line to be printed when you are pressured for time. Or the maitre d' who ensures you get the best table at the restaurant where you are meeting to discuss your proposal with a decision maker.

Secretaries can do very important downfield blocking for you. They can often manage exactly *when* a proposal is seen by a decision maker. For example, a secretary may, at your request, place your proposal on the decision maker's desk along with an affirmative memo, a glowing report, or general good news.

A secretary can advise you when a meeting with the decision maker would coincide with his or her being in a good mood. I know several managers who regularly call the secretary of the boss to ascertain his or her humor before attempting a spontaneous meeting!

In the space below, list the individuals who may be helpful to you by providing resources or favors associated with your goal. Beside each name, indicate the manner in which he or she can aid you in achieving your goal, i.e. your assignment for that person.

FINAL LIST OF ADVOCATES

Name   **Assignment**

12

PRESENTING YOUR PROPOSAL

Take care of the sense and the words will take care of themselves.

—Lewis Carroll

A highly successful marketing executive once said, "When it comes to selling, if you've done your homework, the final exam is a piece of cake!" Admittedly an overstatement, it holds a measure of truth. If you have mapped the mental terrain of the key decision makers and the organization, maintained cognizance of your own needs, and constructed a marketing strategy using your assessment as the mortar between the bricks of your proposal, the actual presentation should hold few surprises.

A major tactical consideration is how you actually present your proposal. The presentation is the recital for all the careful orchestration you have managed thus far. It brings together your array of tactics to produce goal achievement. Analogous to the activities of the advertising unit and sales force in a typical organization, your presentation is the point of contact with the consumer.

The intent of this chapter is to provide tips and techniques which you can use to bolster your confidence and heighten your competence with marketing "on stage." The ideas to come are distilled from many fields—selling, public speaking, power tactics, communication, and adult learning. Choose what works for you!

GETTING YOURSELF READY

You are the most important part of a successful presentation. But we often put so much energy into preparing the proposal and setting up for the presentation, that we forget to get ourselves ready. Let's devote a few minutes to ways you can get into the spirit of greatness!

One area of concern may be how to handle nervousness. Making presentations, particularly those we feel very strongly about, can sometimes causes us unusual anxiety. Our nervousness can be grounded in a fear of failure, a fear of rejection, or simply a fear of the unknown.

Here are a few strategies for dealing with nervousness.

1. *Arrive early.* If possible, arriving one hour early can help assure you that no gremlins have slipped into your meeting room to leave it in disarray after setup. (Obviously, if you are to present your proposal in your boss's office, this would not apply.) Then, take a walk, practice deep breathing, or do anything else that helps you reduce internal stress.

2. *Do not memorize.* A good presenter is one who operates out of knowledge rather than memory. If you depend on remembering every line or every point, one stumble can risk its all coming unraveled. Know your proposal well enough to operate out of conscious competence, that is, knowing your material *and* knowing you know it. Conscious competence is confidence. If you must memorize something, memorize your opening line! Your first five minutes, when nervousness is likely to be at its peak, should feel thoroughly prepared and comfortable for you.

3. *Try acknowledging your nervousness.* Sometimes stage fright is aggravated by trying to hide it. Decision makers are generally astute enough to recognize fear when they see it. If you acknowledge you're a little bit nervous at the outset, not only does this confirm your authenticity, but you can rechannel the energy you'd waste hiding nervousness into managing your proposal presentation more effectively.

4. *Give yourself a break.* If you find your legs quivering or you are short of breath, find a place to pause, reach for a cup of water, take several deep breaths.

5. *Be authentic.* By this, I mean simply be yourself. Live your lines, don't learn your lines. This is not the occasion to decide you'd like to try to emulate your boss, your therapist, or your favorite speaker! If you act out a role, you are making yourself, not your proposal, the center of attention. Try to enjoy the presentation as much as you can.

Nervousness can be your friend. It can help sharpen your thinking and turn your energy to the point you can be as brilliant as you are capable of being. The trick is to turn nervous energy from a distracting to a helping force. Remember, nervousness is not to be avoided, it is to be rechanneled.

THE WIZARD OF ID
by Brant parker and Johnny hart

By permission of Johnny Hart and Field Enterprises, Inc.

PLUGGING INTO DECISION MAKER FREQUENCY

It is essential you avoid getting on the plane of right and wrong. By this, I mean, the moment you attempt to push the decision makers into making what you consider to be the *right* decision, you will likely get buyer resistance. Your objective is not to be right, it is to be effective! Being right is a solo act; being effective is symbiotic. Effectiveness comes by being responsive to where the decision maker *is*, and what the decision maker desires.

Keep in mind that a decision to approve will occur only if the majority of the decision makers perceive (consciously or subconsciously) some direct or indirect personal benefit. Your presentation should be pitched to the personal needs you diagnosed for your audience. As the presentation proceeds, keep asking yourself, "What can I say or do to assist Mr./Ms. X in feeling that approval is to his or her advantage?"

The more you remain plugged into the decision maker's interests, the more you minimize the possibility of resistance. Resistance occurs when people feel coerced, pushed, or controlled. If you sense resistance, back off! Never resist resistance! Defending your proposal will only fuel more resistance. Instead, use problem-solving questions. Where is the resistance focused? Try to determine where the pressure points are on the decision maker. If you accept resistance as a normal reaction to the decision maker's perception of losing control and act so as to remove the pressure, you can redirect his or her energy to your advantage.

SETTING THE CLIMATE

The first few minutes of your presentation are the most crucial. They establish the mental set and give you the opportunity to get the buyers in tune with your goal. Your task is to make the climate of the meeting as pleasant and productive as possible for all. How you stage your opening remarks may, in fact, determine the outcome of your entire proposal presentation.

The following ideas may help you create a climate which will be productive and successful.

1. *Start on time.* Decision makers usually expect it.

2. *Describe your goals* for the meeting and provide a sense of how your time will be managed. Decision makers generally appreciate knowing from the start where the presentation is going, how you envision getting there, and what you expect them to do at the end.

3. *Say how you prefer to handle questions.* You may choose to hold questions until the end to maintain the momentum of the meeting. You may prefer that decision makers ask questions as they occur to them. Decide what works for you and let your audience know at the beginning how you prefer to handle questions.

There are other ways to foster a climate or mental set that will work to your advantage. Essentially, you are attempting to adequately answer these key questions in the mind of the decision maker: why you are there (purpose), what will occur (agenda), what it will mean to the decision maker (payoff), and how you would like the mood to feel and the interaction to occur (attitude). It may be necessary to identify who you are, your role, if some in the room are not familiar with you. As other climate setting ideas occur to you, jot them down in the space below.

CLIMATE-SETTING IDEAS

Having planned how you will set the climate, lay out the crucial elements in your presentation. List the points you wish to make, positive and negative. Then, scrutinize your list carefully to make sure each point is important to your goal; trim from your list all the points which are not.

Go over your list of points a second time and identify which are most likely to be important to the decision makers. These are the points you will want to highlight. Give thought to how much time you will require to cover your points effectively, given the total time you have available. Decide which points might be best left for a discussion period.

TWENTY PRESENTATION TECHNIQUES

There are many fine publications on the techniques of presentation. Here are just a few of the important do's and don'ts which are occasionally forgotten—and which are essential to effective communication with a single decision maker or a group.

1. *Avoid jargon, buzz words, and cliches.* Peter Drucker calls them "the arrogance of the uninformed." *Behavior modification* sounds like a Nazi plot, and *intervention* sounds like something that should be legalized between consenting adults.

2. *Watch out for distracting mannerisms* like clearing your throat, jingling pocket change, or playing with a pointer or felt tip marker.

3. *Don't take yourself too seriously.* If you acknowledge your humanness, the decision makers will follow suit.

4. *Maintain eye contact with your audience.*

5. *Once you adequately cover a point related to your proposal, summarize it, and move quickly on.* Restate essential points frequently to reinforce the continuity of your presentation design.

6. *Use pauses* to let an important point sink in or to encourage reaction.

7. *Avoid distracting body language,* such as shifting your weight from one foot to another, or constantly folding and unfolding your arms. Keep your hands away from your face.

8. *Never make excuses* for any element missing from your presentation, or visual aids not up to par. Excuses call unnecessary attention to imperfections.

9. *Find ways to use humor or anecdotes* to illustrate or underscore important points.

10. *If you are sitting down while making your presentation, sit still* and don't wiggle around.

11. *Try not to hesitate* when you are answering a question.

12. *Listen to the decision makers* and look like you are listening.

13. *Listen to yourself on a tape recorder* in order to eliminate conversational crutches such as "uh," "OK," and "you know."

14. *Know in advance who will be in the proposal presentation meeting and what the pecking order is.* If you sell only to the senior person, you do it at your own peril. The senior person will know he or she is senior and will admire your bringing the junior people into the meeting.

15. *Avoid using more time than allotted.* Rehearse to get an idea of how much time your presentation requires. In the actual presentation, it is likely the content will "spread" as the group interacts with it. A presentation that is fifteen minutes short seldom bothers anyone. One that runs overtime may upset everybody.

16. *In answering questions, answer the thrust of the question as well as its specifics.*

17. *Rehearse answers to probable questions.*

18. *Defer your closing until you feel confident the decision makers have enough information to make a thoughtful decision on your proposal or recommendation.*

19. *Keep your feedback to decision makers nonjudgmental and noncritical* if they request feedback during your presentation or discussion. People never get angry at the speedometer (feedback), only at the cop who gives them the ticket (judgment). (I realize this is easier said than done.)

20. *Talk in the language of your decision makers.* Learn to talk in terms of return on investment (ROI) to relate your goal to the financial value system. Speculate on the ROI if you can't measure it. A 20 percent return sounds too much like a ballpark estimate; 23 percent sounds like you know what you are talking about! Remember that, in all probability, you're selling overhead or a direct expense to profit- and growth-conscious executives.

These twenty tips can help enhance your presentation. There are many others. As you recall or discover others through your experience, write them down in the space provided on the next page.

ADDITIONAL PRESENTATION IDEAS

ADVOCATE POWER

In chapter 11, we explored the use of advocates. If the advocate happens to be a member of the decision-making group, for example, you can encourage that advocate to ask a supportive question, make complimentary remarks, and generally encourage other decision makers to approve the goal. It may be that an advocate could conduct the presentation more effectively than you. Or you may ask an advocate to introduce related data in an earlier meeting, which lays the groundwork for your proposal, idea, or recommendation.

A friend of mine was scheduled to present a proposal to the executive committee of a large association requesting more staff and a larger budget for training. He persuaded a member of the executive committee to use the time just before him on the schedule to present a report from the personnel department; the report indicated the major reason new management recruits resigned was the lack of adequate training. The new training program went into effect that spring.

I once scheduled a meeting with my boss to request approval to pilot-test a new productivity program. Prior to the meeting, I asked a senior executive who was quite enthusiastic about the results from a workshop conducted by my department to call my boss and give him the feedback at 11:15 A.M. The call came right on schedule, fifteen minutes before my meeting on the pilot program, and "greased the skids" to approval.

Use the space below to outline specific ways you might be able to use advocates during the proposed presentation.

**WAYS ADVOCATES CAN HELP
DURING THE PRESENTATION**

WRAPPING IT ALL UP

Much can be said for that assertive, confident energy we label charisma. If you have it, by all means use it. Yet, it is important to remember that effective proposal presentations are those which capture and transmit an authenticity and realness to the audience. Hold on to your uniqueness while you plan and conduct your proposal presentation—relax and enjoy yourself—and you're bound to be successful.

Before bidding farewell, return to page 130 and complete Section B of your Influence Plan form. You may also want to review your initial aim (page 16) to determine its appropriateness at this point in accomplishing one or more of your objectives.

POSTSCRIPT: DEALING WITH THE DECISION

The presentation ends and, at some point, the die is cast. I hope you get many "yes" decisions on your proposals, ideas, requests, or recommendations. If the vote is thumbs down, analyze the process you used, to determine whether choosing a different path would have led you to a different clearing. You may decide that, in retrospect, it was not a game that could have been won and you did your best. Pat yourself on the back!

The process of influencing does not end with a green light; it is an ongoing process. In our influencing model, the final step, Step 13, is to cycle back to the beginning, reassessing your goal or beginning anew. If the decision was not a favorable one, take time to debrief yourself, methodically rechecking each step. We all learn early in life that it is important to profit from our mistakes. We also learn that such profit-taking only comes after a disciplined look at exactly what we did. After rechecking, begin the influencing process again.

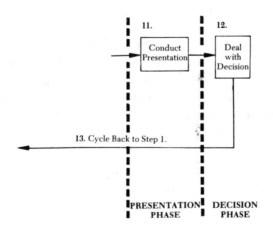

ROMANCING THE SALE

A favorable decision is worthy of your celebrating your success. Having done so, it is time to "romance the sale," to prevent the onslaught of "buyer's blues." Buyer's blues is the label for the feeling many of us get after making some major decisions. We buy a new house or car and then wonder whether we really got a good deal. We select a college or an employer and, possibly, have early second thoughts.

Buyer's blues do not always occur, but they happen frequently enough to conclude that the phenomenon is fairly normal. Your task following a positive decision is to do whatever is required to confirm in the mind of the decision maker that approval was the correct decision. Romancing the decision requires further planning and action on your part.

Ford Motor Company provides its new car buyers with a subscription to a colorful magazine about interesting places to travel in their new automobiles. Marriott Hotels give you a special card after your fifth stay that entitles you to many extras, including no wait check-in. Many airlines offer free flights or upgraded seat status to their frequent flyers. All are aimed to say to their customers, "You were wise to select our product or service."

The Role of Evaluation

An important post-decision action is to evaluate the effect of the decision. There are many approaches to evaluation. One I have found to be particularly relevant to the influencing process is a set of questions developed by Tony Putman.[19] He calls them "guide questions" and presents them as the primary focus for a "pragmatic evaluation."

1. *What are the results of the evaluation intended to be used for?* The results of your evaluation are designed to enable some person or persons (the decision maker) to decide about the effect of your goal. The more precise your answer to this key question, the more focused your results can be.

---

[19]Anthony O. Putman, "Pragmatic Evaluation," *Training and Development Journal* 34, no. 10 (October 1980): 36-48.

2. *What kind of information counts with the decision maker?* We earlier described the importance of presenting your proposal in the *form* most meaningful to the decision maker. The same applies to evaluation data. Anecdotal data on your behalf from people whose views matter to the decision maker may be far more forceful in romancing a sale than all the statistical analyses in the world. On the other hand, your decision maker may value detailed status reports with numeric justification. Consider such efforts to all be part of your ongoing influencing process. If the boss wants chi-squares and multiple regression analyses, deliver them with confidence. Your belief in the worth of the decision will be contagious.

Some other important considerations are:

3. *What shall I assess to get that kind of information?*

4. *Whose cooperation, sanction, or approval is needed to do the evaluation?*

5. *How shall I collect, analyze, and use the data?*

The evaluation data you produce can be useful to you in two ways: as a means of doing a "Monday-morning quarterback's" analysis of your process, and as a means to assure decision makers of the rightness of their decision.

Advertise your successes. Share your glory or success with the sponsoring decision makers. Don't forget, however, to openly acknowledge your failures. (By the same token, don't have too many failures by fighting battles you cannot win.)

Advocates should be actively involved. They can be extremely helpful in aiding you to romance the sale. Express your gratitude to the decision makers for their approval. Too frequently, sellers forget to thank the buyer for the business, or friends for valued recommendations.

Plan now for your next influencing effort. What supporting data might you need? Begin collecting it now. Like saving cancelled checks for that one-in-a-hundred chance of a tax audit, consider every program or activity as some day requiring in-depth justification by the decision makers.

Are there new advocates instrumental in your future efforts whom you should begin getting to know? Can you plan methods for updating your assessment of the needs of the organization? What resources do you have that need bolstering or overhauling? What staff members need redirection, guidance, or leadership for greater contribution in future influencing efforts?

LOOKING FORWARD

Peter Vaill has for several years studied the characteristics of high-performing individuals and units.[20] In his view, the major ingredient in high performance is the act of "purposing"—the perpetual effort to keep output aligned with mission.

Your goal as a professional is to achieve results, the output of performance. A part of superior performance entails the effective influencing of others. The number one means to accomplishing that dimension of your performance is keeping your goal in sync with the role and mission of the organization.

The first step is attaining a broader perspective on how influencing happens and tailoring your actions to fit that perspective. This book has unfolded a perspective along with suggested tools and techniques. Tailoring the techniques entails further introspection and innovation; perfecting them requires perspiration and patience—all grounded in "purposing."

We began this working book with an examination of the role of alignment in effective influencing. I want to end by focusing on a related ingredient—eligibility.

Influencing at its most basic level is the act of encouraging change. If conditions were as you desired, you would have little need to make them different—to change. Stated differently, your role as an influencer is in reality the role of change agent.

An important lesson I have learned about change agentry is this: I am not likely to change a person's perception unless I demonstrate to that person that I understand and appreciate (that's different from *agree with*) the person's current perception. Demonstration of that understanding and appreciation is the key to being *eligible* to foster a change. Granted, you can con folks into change. But consider the many stories in the marketing literature pointing up the disasters resulting from this approach, the deserved reputations of the "snake oil salespeople." The risks far outweigh the gains.

Alignment with organizational mission increases your eligibility. Understanding and appreciating the needs and desires of the buyer and the marketplace increase your eligibility. Decision makers

---

[20]Peter B. Vaill is Professor of Human Systems, Department of Management Science, School of Government and Business Administration, The George Washington University, in Washington, D.C. His first work on high-performing systems appeared in *Leadership: Where Else Can We Go?*, edited by Morgan W. McCall and Michael M. Lombardo, Durham, NC: Duke University Press, 1978, pp. 103-125.

approve proposals for the same reasons consumers make purchases—a belief that the seller has understood their needs and desires and offers a product or service, a proposal or idea, which will be a route to satisfaction.

You are on your way to being more effective as an influencer. I wish you success and satisfaction with the buyers in your organizational marketplace.

ONLY CONNECT!

ADDITIONAL RESOURCES

Ackoff, Russell L. *A Concept of Corporate Planning*. New York: Wiley Interscience, 1970.

Bell, Chip R. "Energize Your Staff to Improve Productivity," *Management Review* 71, no. 2 (February 1982): 46-51.

Bell, Chip R. "How to Market Training within Your Organization," *Training*, February 1977, pp. 32-35.

Bell, Chip R. "Selling: Persuasion or Manipulation?" *Xchange* (Xerox Learning Systems), no. 3 (1976), p. 5.

Bell, Chip R. & Fredric H. Margolis. *A Presenter's Guide to Conferences*. Washington, D.C.: American Society for Training and Development, 1980.

Bell, Chip R. & Leonard Nadler (eds.). *The Client-Consultant Handbook*. Houston: Gulf Publishing, 1979.

Block, Peter. *Flawless Consulting*. Austin, Tex.: Learning Concepts, 1981.

Burns, James MacGregor. *Leadership*. New York: Harper & Row, 1978.

Buzzotta, Victor R., R.E. Lefton, & Manual Sherber. *Effective Selling through Psychology*. New York: Wiley Interscience, 1972.

Corey, E. Raymond & Steven H. Star. *Organization Strategy: A Marketing Approach*. Boston: Harvard Business School, 1971.

Culbert, Samuel A. *The Organization Trap*. New York: Basic Books, 1974.

Downing, George D. *Basic Marketing*. Columbus, Ohio: Charles E. Merrill, 1971.

Drucker, Peter F. *Management: Tasks, Responsibilities, Practices*. New York: Harper & Row, 1973.

Drucker, Peter F. *Concept of the Corporation*. New York: John Day, 1972.

Drucker, Peter F. *Managing for Results*. New York: Harper & Row, 1964.

Hanan, Mack, J. Cribbin, and H. Heiser. *Consultative Selling*. New York: AMACOM, 1970.

Jay, Antony. *Effective Presentation*. London: British Institute of Management, 1972.

Kotler, Philip. "From Sales Obsession to Marketing Effectiveness," *Harvard Business Review*, November/December 1977, pp. 75-76.

Kotler, Philip. *Marketing Management*. Englewood Cliffs, N.J.: Prentice-Hall, 1976.

Levitt, Theodore. "Marketing Myopia," *Harvard Business Review*, September/October 1975, p. 26.

Levitt, Theodore. *Marketing for Business Growth*. New York: McGraw-Hill, 1969.

Levitt, Theodore. *Innovation in Marketing*. New York: McGraw-Hill, 1962.

Levitt, Theodore. "Marketing Myopia," *Harvard Business Review*, July/August 1960, p. 45.

Myers, Isabel Briggs. *Gifts Differing*. Palo Alto, Calif.: Consulting Psychologists Press, 1980.

Porter, Michael E. *Competitive Strategy*. New York: The Free Press, 1980.

Reddin, W.J. *Effective Management by Objectives*. New York: McGraw-Hill, 1971.

Roger, David C.D. *Corporate Strategy and Long-Range Planning*. Ann Arbor, Mich.: The Landis Press, 1973.

Runyon, Kenneth E. *Consumer Behavior and the Practice of Marketing*. Columbus, Ohio: Charles E. Merrill, 1977.

Schutz, William C. *The Interpersonal Underworld (FIRO)*. Palo Alto, Calif.: Science & Behavior Books, 1966.

Steele, Fritz. *The Feel of the Workplace*. Reading, Mass: Addison-Wesley, 1977.

Steiner, George A. *Top Management Planning*. New York: Macmillan, 1969.

Tregoe, Benjamin B. & John W. Zimmerman. *Top Management Strategy*. New York: Simon & Schuster, 1980.

Wilson, Aubrey. *The Marketing of Professional Services*. New York: McGraw-Hill, 1972.

ACKNOWLEDGEMENTS

I wish to acknowledge several people whose support, advice, and encouragement enabled me to complete this book.

First, to Nancy R. Bell, whose love, patience, and compassionate critique made the task more joyful and the output complete. She frequently "took up the slack" to provide me valuable space for focus on the book.

Second, to Bruce W. Fritch, a world-class marketing consultant whose creative viewpoint is woven throughout this book. Bruce was my marketing advisor when I encountered conceptual obstacles, my writing expert when my rough words needed polish, and my close friend throughout.

Leslie Stephen was the ideal editor, balancing supportive attention with work freedom. Her superb craftsmanship made ideas sound wonderful. Ellen Suite typed the manuscript over and over and over—all the while telling me how much she liked what she was typing. Finally, to Larry N. Davis, Ray Bard, and Charles Peers for their initial interest and belief in this book.

To all of you, my heartfelt thanks.

ABOUT THE AUTHOR

Chip R. Bell is an independent consultant based in Charlotte, North Carolina, where he specializes in trainer development, leadership training, and organization-improvement consulting. In addition, he is a director of Androgogy Press, a publishing company in Austin, Texas, that specializes in short, adult-learning-based, packaged training programs. Formerly, he served as a principal with LEAD Associates, Inc., a training and consulting firm in Charlotte; a vice president and director of management development and training for NCNB Corporation, a large, one-bank holding company; and a staff member of the Department of Instruction, U.S. Army Infantry School.

A nationally known trainer, he is the co-author of *The Client-Consultant Handbook* and *A Presenter's Guide to Conferences*. His articles have appeared in such professional publications as *Management Review, Training and Development Journal, Personnel Journal, Personnel Administrator, Educational Technology, Data Training, Northeast Training News,* and *Journal of European Training*. He is a member of the American Society for Training and Development, the American Society of Personnel Administration, and the World Future Society, and he holds a doctorate in human resource development from The George Washington University.